WHITE ROOTS OF PEACE

THE IROQUOIS BOOK OF LIFE
WHITE ROOTS OF PEACE

Paul A.W. Wallace
Illustrated by John Kahionhes Fadden
Foreword by Chief Leon Shenandoah
Epilogue by John Mohawk

Clear Light Publishers
Santa Fe, New Mexico

Library of Congress Cataloging-in-Publication Data

Wallace, Paul A.W.
    White Roots of peace: the Iroquois book of life / Paul A.W. Wallace: foreword by Chief Leon Shenandoah : epilogue by John Mohawk.
        p. cm.
Originaly published : Philadelphia: University of Pennsylvania Press, 1946.

    ISBN 0-940666- 36-7
    1. Iroquois Indians, 2. Iroquois Indians - Legends I. Title
Ee99.17W26 1994
970.004'97 - dc20   93-24297
                                                      CIP

Printed in the U.S.A.

Cover painting: *Tree of Peace* by Chief Oren Lyons.
Cover drawing: *The Washington Covenant Belt,* which was used as a covenant of peace between the thirteen original colonies and the Iroquois Confederacy.

 Printed on Recycled Paper

To
the memory of
(Chief William D. Loft)
DEWASERAGE
who held the Mohawk name and title of
SHARENKHOWANE
in the Council of the Six Nations

and
to the Tadodahos who carry the vision
of the Peacemaker
from generation to generation

PUBLISHER'S
ACKNOWLEDGMENT

In January of 1946, when The White Roots of Peace *was first published, Paul A. W. Wallace wrote:*

> *It was the late Chief William D. Loft of the Six Nations Reserve, a Mohawk artist and scholar of distinction, who first inspired me with the desire to probe under the surface of the Deganawidah legend, which he had told to me. In his own person Chief Loft exemplified Deganawidah's message of Peace and Power.*

In introducing this new edition, we would like to extend our acknowledgment to the late Paul Wallace himself, for his vison and his tireless efforts to pass on the story of Deganawidah and the Iroquois Confederacy. We would also like to thank historian John Mohawk, who, drawing on his vast knowledge, has taken up the story where Paul Wallace left off; John Kahionhes Fadden for artwork that compellingly expresses the spirit of the Confederacy and the Peacemaker; Chief Oren Lyons for his continuing inspiration and advice; Murray Heller for his contribution to keeping this work alive; Kusumita Peterson, who first brought it to our attention.

And Chief Leon Shenandoah for adding his words to this book, and not least, for being who he is.

Harmon Houghton, Publisher

CONTENTS

Chief Leon Shenandoah,
Tadodaho
Fall 1967 to present

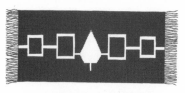

FOREWORD
Chief Leon Shenandoah

THE PEACEMAKER *came a long time ago—before the Europeans came. It happened at a time when there was great conflict among the Indian nations living here—from north of Lake Ontario and all through the Finger Lakes and the Mohawk River to the Niagara River. It was a civil war.*

There was already a prediction that something would happen, that when there was a time of great trouble a messenger would come from the place of our Creator to help the people. Our Peacemaker was born among the people north of Lake Ontario, near the Bay of Quinte. He was Huron, and it is said his birth was attended by unusual circumstances which suggested spiritual powers were present. It is said his message of peace and a good mind was sent from the one who created the human beings—our Creator.

When he was a young man, he began talking about

bringing peace to all the nations, but his own people rejected his message. Then he journeyed among the Mohawk, and eventually he found people—leaders—who were willing to listen and to take hold of what he was trying to teach.

Everywhere people were abusing one another—ambushing innocent people on the trails in the forest, attacking people in fishing camps, and even in the towns. It was said that women and children bore scars from these endless conflicts. Assassinations were common. Some of the worst of the warrior leaders were even said to commit cannibalism upon their enemies, almost as if they were hunting humans for food. It was a very bad time.

The Peacemaker came to the Mohawk looking for some of the leaders—war chiefs—who were responsible for continuing this violence. He found some of these leaders—assassins, cannibals, a lot of bad people at first—who were willing to listen to his words and to become sane human beings who possessed healthy minds. There were nine of them among the Mohawk. While he was in the Mohawk country he summoned to his side an Onondaga chief who had abandoned society and had gone to live in the forest in self-imposed exile because his daughters had all been killed through assasinations and sorcery. His name was Ayowenta, and this is where the English name Hiawatha comes from, although the poem about Hiawatha has nothing to do with this story. Ayowenta became the Peacemaker's loyal companion and assistant in promoting what would become the Great Law. Our memory of Ayowenta is different in some ways from Wallace's account.

The Peacemaker then journeyed to the Oneida, and the same thing happened that had happened among the Mohawk. He found leaders and persuaded them that violence could be replaced with thinking, and they, like the Mohawk, said that if the other nations would take hold of this proposal, this law, that they would join. Eventually, there were nine Oneida leaders who followed him.

When he came to the Onondaga, most of the leaders listened and agreed to his plan, but there was one who did not. His name was Tadodaho, and he was a very powerful and stubborn man. The Peacemaker spent some time at Onondaga, but he made no progress with Tadodaho. After a time he went among the Cayuga with his message of peace, and again the leaders agreed to his plan. Then he went to the Seneca and, after a difficult time, the Seneca also joined the plan for a new order. The Seneca were the largest of the original Five Nations, and they had a great many warriors.

Now all of the Five Nations had embraced the plan for peace and a good mind on the earth except for one Onondaga chief—Tadodaho. All efforts at persuasion failed. Finally, a woman called the Peacemaker and Ayowenta to her lodge. She was a powerful and respected woman among a people who live west of the Genesee, and her name was Jikonhsaseh. She was the first woman to embrace the message of peace and good tidings, and she is called the Mother of Nations or the Peace Queen because she had a plan to bring Tadodaho under the Great Peace.

The Peacemaker and his followers journeyed to Onondaga to find Tadodaho. They discovered him in a swamp—a rough, dirty place. His appearance, they said, was very frightening. Snakes were woven in his hair, and his body appeared crooked and misshapen, and everything about him was unpleasant to behold. The expression on his face let the people know he was unbearably cruel.

The journey to approach Tadodaho took a long time. The Cayuga had joined this crusade, and they were singing a song which was provided especially for this meeting. When he heard that song, Tadodaho felt at first threatened. But it was the song that turned him; and he melted when he heard that song. He agreed to listen to them. He had long been the worst human being in the world, so terrible that the people had said, "the mind in that body is not the mind of a human being." And he was the last to reform, but they were able to comb the snakes from his hair and to transform his mind using songs and words to bring him health and peace. Jikonshaseh had told them to use songs and words to transform his mind, and that he would become the leader—like the facilitator—of the

12

Grand Council. That is the story of the remarkable leader of the Haudenosaunee—the Six Nations. His title has been handed down from generation to generation, like the title of Dalai Lama or Pope. I am Tadodaho today.

When an individual who holds the title of Tadodaho passes away, another is raised up in his place and the tradition goes on. The Onondaga Council selects Tadodaho, and it is a great responsibility. Tadodaho represents the mind which promotes peace and the welfare of all people. He must be kind to the people and express love for their welfare, and he must never hurt anybody.

When I was small, creeping on the floor, two women were working at the stove and they accidentally spilled hot water over me. It almost took my life, and my mother had to go around to get medicine. They never took me to the hospital. Instead, they took me to a Seneca man, and they held a sacred ceremony which can cure illness. At that ceremony an old man stood up and said, "You are that boy!" I was there because the ceremony was for me, and the old man said, "That boy, when he grows up, he will have a high position that will have to do with a lot of people." This happened when I was a small child, and I remember still today.

It was already decided, when I was young, what I am doing today. My mother didn't say anything, but that's probably why she pushed me along this path. We made a special point of going to ceremonies. When there was a

13

ceremony in the longhouse, I wouldn't go to school. My mother said, "You're not going to school. You're going to the ceremony." That made me glad. I didn't like school. So I grew up going to the ceremonies all the time, and in time I learned how to run the ceremonies and to be in charge. And now it is getting to be a time when someone else must learn and take over from here.

When I was young and I first began to listen to the chiefs, one of the two men I have known in this lifetime who held the title of Tadodaho stood at council and said, "You must watch what we are doing and listen to what we say. Someday we will not be around and others must succeed us." He met with the group I was with, and it sounded like he was talking to me. Since then I have tried to live that way—as though he were talking to me.

The teachings are very good. The most important thing is that each individual must treat all others, all the people who walk on Mother Earth, including every nationality, with kindness. That covers a lot of ground. It doesn't apply only to my people. I must treat everyone I meet the same. When people turn their thoughts to the Creator, they give the Creator the power to enter their minds and to bring good thoughts. The most difficult part of this is that the Creator desired that there be no bloodshed among human beings and that there be peace, good relations, and always a good mind. It is difficult because people criticize the leaders all the time. But a

14

leader must have seven layers of skin so those words don't penetrate and cause him to think thoughts which are not in the interest of peace and the well-being of everyone.

I see the Peacemaker as a man of peace, but with the power to do good things. When he was alive, as he moved about on the earth, he was getting his instructions from the spiritual powers. It is the same today. I try to tell people that as you are walking about, and you think you are using the good mind, the Creator is talking to you, coming into your mind. You think it's your own mind, but words are being put in and you're not aware. And sometimes there are the thoughts of another mind, the mind that would destroy life. That was the mind which had possessed Tadodaho before the transformation, before he embraced the Good Mind and became a leader of the Grand Council. His transformation was complete, and he became a spokesman for peace and righteousness. His is one of the great stories of all time.

THE FIVE NATIONS

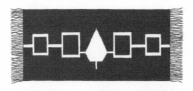

FAITH AND FIRE

THIS IS THE STORY *of the founding at Onondaga (Syracuse, New York), some time about the middle of the fifteenth century, of the United Nations of the Iroquois, the famous Indian Confederacy that provided a model for, and an incentive to, the transformation of the thirteen colonies into the United States of America.*

"It would be a strange thing," wrote Benjamin Franklin, "if Six Nations of ignorant savages should be capable of forming a scheme for such a union, and be able to execute it in such a manner as that it has subsisted ages and appears indissoluble; and yet that a like union should be impracticable for ten or a dozen English colonies to whom it is more necessary and must be more advantageous, and who cannot be supposed to want an equal understanding of their interests."

In Franklin's day the Six Nations, as the Iroquois then called themselves, were the greatest Indian power on the American continent. The original Five Nations—Mo-

19

hawks, Oneidas, Onondagas, Cayugas, and Senecas, with whom a sixth, the Tuscaroras, had been joined since about 1710—dominated all surrounding tribes, and, from their homeland in northern New York, between the Hudson and Niagara rivers, maintained a pax iroquoia that in their most heroic days had extended from what is now New England to the Illinois region and from the Ottawa River to Chesapeake Bay.

It was not by force alone that the Iroquois held this vast region under their peace. It was by statesmanship, by a profound understanding of the principles of peace itself. They knew that any real peace must be based on justice and a healthy reasonableness. They knew also that peace will endure only if men recognize the sovereignty of a common law and are prepared to back that law with force—not chiefly for the purpose of punishing those who have disturbed the peace, but rather for the purpose of preventing such disturbance by letting all men know, in advance of any contingency, that the law will certainly prevail.

Behind their statesmanship lay a will to peace among the people, without which all the wisdom of their chiefs gathered in the Great Council at Onondaga would have been futile. It was in the handling of this problem, how to maintain a popular will to peace, that the Iroquois made their greatest contribution to government—a contribution that it may be profitable for us to examine today, since there is now no greater problem confronting global states-manship than that of maintaining this popular will to peace despite increasing tensions in an ever-more-narrowly-jostling world society.

Among the Five Nations it is evident that the peace incentive was a complex thing, rooted in many motives, chief among which were three: the example of two culture heroes, a unique interpretation of the meaning of peace itself, and a set of peace symbols that seized the imagination and so gave both interpretation and example a power to drive the human will.

The two culture heroes, whose deeds and words have been treasured through the centuries in a traditional narrative of great beauty, were two men of peace, Deganawídah[*] and his spokesman, Hiawatha.

Deganawidah, a Huron Indian by birth but a Mohawk by adoption, was the man of faith, the man of purpose, who gave a New Mind and a new way of life to his people. His name, it is believed by some, means the Master of Things, for he implemented his visions with a machinery of government that gave them substance.

Hiawatha, an Onondaga Indian by birth but like Deganawidah a Mohawk by adoption, was the man of fire,

---

[*] An accent is added on the first mention of names to aid in pronunciation.

21

the man of feeling, whose eloquence won converts to Deganawidah's visions. His name means He Who Combs, for he combed the twists out of men's perverted minds.

Dewaseráge (Chief William D. Loft), the Mohawk scholar to whom so much in this book is owing, has expressed the opinion that the name Deganawidah means "Double Row of Teeth" and that this appellation explains the physical impediment that caused Deganawidah to appoint Hiawatha to speak for him.

Hiawatha, the poet, is popularly believed to have invented wampum, that substitute for writing made of small shell beads threaded in symbolic designs on strings or belts, and with it to have instituted the beautiful mourning and other council rituals of the Iroquois. Deganawidah, the man of legal mind, gave his people a constitution. Together they were, as Dr. Arthur C. Parker, descendant of an ancient Seneca family, calls them, "the Blackstones of their people," who invested the customs of five distinct nations with the power of law, and brought these nations into a union cemented by such powerful sanctions of law, custom, and religion as served to make it all but indestructible.

"Through the law as a guiding force," writes Dr. Parker, "and through the heroes as ideals, the Iroquois have persisted as a people."

The task of disentangling fact from folklore in the story of these heroes is not attempted here. No effort is made to distinguish between what the Iroquois actually received from Deganawidah and Hiawatha while they lived and what the popular imagination after their death gave back by way of tribute to their memory. For of course these culture heroes, as we see them now in the legend, are in part the product of imaginative processes which their living originals had set in motion.

The purpose in these pages is to show the legend in its dynamic unity: to let it appear as the constructive force it actually was, one that seized on the minds of the Iroquois, directed their moral energies to the preservation of the Peace, and so gave them an influence on history out of all proportion to their numbers.

The story of Deganawidah and Hiawatha virtually constituted the Iroquois Bible. In it, if anywhere, are to be found the moral incentives that enabled them to make their Great Peace lasting.

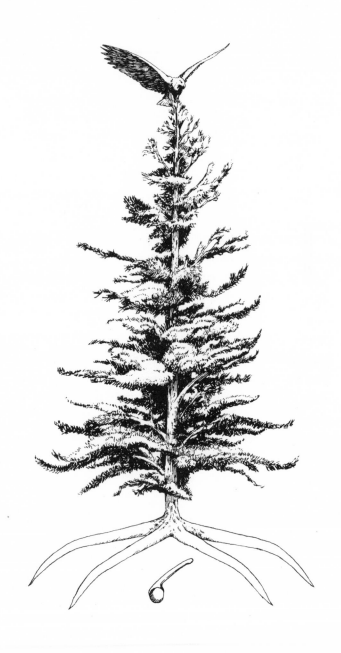

THE TREE OF PEACE

THE INDIANS OF THE *Five Nations were a practical people. They lived in good houses, built walled towns for their protection, and supported themselves by the cultivation of the soil. Corn, beans, and squash, the "Three Sisters," formed the staple of their diet, with venison and fish in season. Their clothing was adequate and modest. They gave themselves steam baths in specially constructed huts by pouring water on heated stones. In war their discipline and skilled leadership made up for lack of numbers. In private life they got on well with one another, their games, dances, and conversation being seldom interrupted by personal quarrels. In public life they excelled in political organization and the forensic arts that went with it.*

They were not, for the most part, of a philosophical turn of mind, their abilities being rather of an Hebraic than of an Hellenic cast. They were better in practice than in theory. Their religion was sounder than their theology, their political institutions maturer than their political science. The only science in which they excelled was that of human relationships.

Nowhere is this practical bent of mind better seen than in the way they talked about peace. Peace was not, as they conceived it, a negative thing, the mere absence of war or an interval between wars, to be recognized only as the stepchild of the law—as unfortunately has been the case with most Western peoples, among whom the laws of peace, in the international field, have been recognized by jurists as an afterthought to the laws of war.

To the Iroquois, peace was the law. They used the same word for both. Peace (the Law) was righteousness in action, the practice of justice between individuals and nations. If they ever recognized it as a mystic presence, like the light which Shelley conceived as giving "grace and truth to life's unquiet dream," they found it, not in some im-agined retreat from the world, but in human institutions, especially in a good government. Their own Confederacy, which they named the Great Peace, was sacred. The chiefs who administered the League were their priests.

In their thought peace was so inseparable from the life of man that they had no separate term by which to denominate it. It was thought of and spoken of in terms of its component elements: as Health and Reason (soundness of body and sanity of mind), Law (justice codified to meet particular cases), and Authority (which gives confidence that justice will prevail).

Peace was a way of life, characterized by wisdom and graciousness.

The root word which, in various combinations, is used to express "peace" in the Iroquois tongue is the same as that used for "noble" and "the Lord" in their translations of the Bible. Peace was to their mind nobility, the Great Good. Even such renderings of the term in English are too ab- stract to catch their way of looking at it. Peace was the Good expressed in action, that is, the good life. It was also, in their thought, the Ideal Commonwealth—not Utopia (No Place), but Kayánerénhkowa (the Great Peace) established so firmly at Onondaga.

Their symbol for this Peace was a tree, and the tree had roots in the earth.

The power of symbols is profound, especially among an active and emotional people; for symbols are a means by which practical persons, shy of metaphysics and im-patient of theory, are enabled to apprehend great ideas, take them to heart, and put them to work. The Iroquois fed their minds and guided their actions by means of symbols. When Deganawidah stood before the first council of the United Nations at Onondaga and planted the Tree of the Great Peace, he planted in the hearts of his people a symbol that was to give power and permanence to their union.

Like the spires on our churches, the Great White Pine

which "pierces the sky" and "reaches the sun" lifted the thoughts of the Iroquois to the meanings of peace—the Good News which they believed the Great Spirit, the Iroquois god Tarachiawágon (Holder of the Heavens), had sent Deganawidah to impart to them.

In general the Tree signified the Law, that is, the constitution, which expressed the terms of their union. But there were other important elements in the symbol.

The Branches signified shelter, the protection and secur-ity that people found in union under the shadow of the Law.

The Roots, which stretched to the four quarters of the earth, signified the extension of the Law, the Peace, to embrace all mankind. Other nations, not yet members of the League, would see these roots as they grew outward, and, if they were people of goodwill, would desire to follow them to their source and take shelter with others under the Tree.

The Eagle That Sees Afar, which Deganawidah placed on the very summit of the Tree, signified watchfulness. "And the meaning of placing an Eagle on the top of the Tree," said Deganawidah, "is to watch the roots which extend to the North and to the South and to the East and to the West, and the Eagle will discover if any evil is approaching your Confederacy, and will scream and give the alarm and all the Nations of the Confederacy at once shall hear the alarm and come to the front."

"The Eagle," said Deganawidah, "shall have your power." It was a reminder to his people that the best

political contrivance that the wit of man can devise is impotent to keep the peace unless a watchful people stands always on guard to defend it.

Then Deganawidah uprooted the Tree and under it disclosed a Cavern through which ran a stream of water, passing out of sight into unknown regions under the earth. Into this current he cast the weapons of war, the hatchets and war-clubs, saying, "We here rid the earth of these things of an Evil Mind." Then, replacing the Tree, "Thus," he said, "shall the Great Peace be established, and hostilities shall no longer be known between the Five Nations, but peace to the United People."

It was a simple but effective symbol he had given them in the Tree of Peace, clear in outline, suggestive, and easily remembered. It was inspiring and yet at the same time it was familiar and friendly to people who knew the forest as their home. To the man of the Five Nations, the pine in the valley through which his trail passed spoke the message of Deganawidah: Hold fast to friends, for in union there is strength; welcome the stranger and give him shelter, for he may become a prop to your house; bury your hates and let them be forgotten, for if old stories are to be revived there can never be an end to war.

And the eagle which the man of the Five Nations saw circling in the sky above him was a reminder that the price of peace, as of liberty, is eternal vigilance.

THE LEGEND
OF DEGANAWIDAH

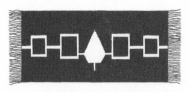

"I AM DEGANAWIDAH"

DEGANAWIDAH IS *said to have been born at a Huron settlement, Tkahaánaye, on the north shore of Lake Ontario not far from the site of modern Kingston, Ontario.*

Before his birth the name of the child was disclosed to his grandmother, as was the way among the Iroquois, in a dream.

A messenger from the Great Spirit stood before the grandmother and said:

"It is the will of the Master of Life, the Holder of the Heavens, that thy daughter, a virgin, shall bear a child. He shall be called Deganawidah, the Master of Things, for he brings with him the Good News of Peace and Power. Care for him well, thou and thy daughter, for he has a great office to perform in the world."

"What is the child's office to be?" asked the grandmother.

"His office is to bring peace and life to the people on

earth," replied the messenger. "After he is grown to manhood, see that thou place no obstacle in his way when he desires to leave home to spread the New Mind among the nations."

So when Deganawidah was become a man, he said one day to his mother and grandmother:

"I shall now build my canoe, for the time has come for me to set out on my mission in the world. Know that far away, on lakes and many rivers, I go seeking the council smoke of nations beyond this lake, holding my course toward the sunrise. It is my business to stop the shedding of blood among human beings."

When he had built his canoe and, with the help of his mother and grandmother, had brought it to the water, he bade them farewell.

"Do not look for me to return," he said, "for I shall not come again this way. Should you wish to know if all is well with me, go to the hilltop yonder where stands a single tree. Cut at the tree with your hatchets, and, if blood flows from the wound, you will know that I have perished and my work has failed. But if no blood flows, all is well, my mission is successful."

"But the canoe is made of stone," said his grandmother. "It will not float."

"It will float," replied Deganawidah. "This shall be a sign that my words are true."

34

He entered the canoe, and it moved swiftly out into the Lake.

Deganawidah crossed Lake Ontario (Sganyadaii-yo, the Beautiful Great Lake) and approached the land of the Iroquois. As the shoreline took form to his eyes, he scanned it for signs of ascending smoke, but saw none; for indeed the settlements at that time were all back among the hills, whose steep sides offered protection to stockaded villages against their enemies. Those were evil days, for the five Iroquois peoples were all at war with one another, and made themselves an easy prey to their fierce Algonquin enemies, the Adirondacks, who came down on them from what is now northern New England, and the Wolves or Mahicans of Hudson's River, who assailed them on the east.

As Deganawidah neared the land, he saw the figures of men, small in the distance, running along the shore; for some hunters had seen a sparkle of light from the white stone canoe and ran to see what it could be. Whereupon Deganawidah turned his canoe toward them, and, making land swiftly, beached the canoe and climbed the bank and stood before them.

Looking about him, he saw that the region was bare of cornfields.

"Is there no settlement here?" he asked.

"No," they replied.

"Then what has brought you to this desolate place?"

35

"We are hunters," they said. "We have come away from our hill settlement because there is strife in it."

"Go back to your settlement," said Deganawidah. "Tell your chief that the Good News of Peace and Power has come, and that there will be no more strife in his village. If he asks whence peace is to come, say to him, 'It will come.' "

"Who art thou that speakest thus to us?"

"I am Deganawidah," he replied. "I come from the west and I go toward the sunrise. I am called Deganawidah in the world."

When he turned and went down the bank to enter his canoe, the men wondered as they looked, for they saw that the canoe was made of white stone.

The hunters, returning to the settlement as Deganawidah had bidden them, went to their chief and said to him, "The Good News of Peace and Power has come."

"What is this you are saying?" said the chief.

"There will be no more strife in the settlement."

"Who told you this?"

They replied, "He is called Deganawidah in the world."

"Where did you see him?"

"On the Beautiful Great Lake. He came from the west and he goes toward the sunrise. His canoe is made of white stone and it moves swiftly."

Then the chief began to wonder at the news. His town was at war, and his people within the stockades were hungry and quarreling among themselves.

38

"Whence can peace come?" he said.

They replied, "It will come."

Then said the chief: "Truly this is a wonderful thing. Such news of itself will bring peace to the settlement if once men believe it. All will be glad and at ease in their minds to know that this thing will be."

So Deganawidah passed from settlement to settlement, finding that men desired peace and would practice it if they knew for a certainty that others would practice it, too.

But first, after leaving the hunters, Deganawidah sought the house of a certain woman who lived by the warriors' path which passed between the east and the west.

When Deganawidah arrived, the woman placed food before him and, after he had eaten, asked him his message.

"I carry the Mind of the Master of Life," he replied, "and my message will bring an end to the wars between east and west."

"How will this be?" asked the woman, who wondered at his words, for it was her custom to feed the warriors passing before her door on their way between the east and the west.

"The Word that I bring," he said, "is that all peoples shall love one another and live together in peace. This message has three parts: Righteousness and Health and Power—

Gáiwoh, Skénon, Gashasdénshaa. *And each part has two branches.*

"Righteousness means justice practiced between men and between nations; it means also a desire to see justice prevail.

"Health means soundness of mind and body; it also means peace, for that is what comes when minds are sane and bodies cared for.

"Power means authority, the authority of law and custom, backed by such force as is necessary to make justice prevail; it means also religion, for justice enforced is the will of the Holder of the Heavens and has his sanction."

"Thy message is good," said the woman; "but a word is nothing until it is given form and set to work in the world. What form shall this message take when it comes to dwell among men?"

"It will take the form of the longhouse," replied Deganawidah, "in which there are many fires, one for each family, yet all live as one household under one chief mother. Hereabouts are five nations, each with its own council fire, yet they shall live together as one household in peace. They shall be the Kanonsiónni, the Longhouse. They shall have one mind and live under one law. Thinking shall replace killing, and there shall be one commonwealth."

"That is indeed a good message," said the woman. "I take hold of it. I embrace it."

"Now it shall come to pass in that Longhouse," said *Deganawidah*, "that the women shall possess the titles of chiefship. They shall name the chiefs. That is because thou, my Mother, wert the first to accept the Good News of Peace and Power. Henceforth thou shalt be called *Jigónhsasee, New Face*, for thy countenance evinces the New Mind, and thou shalt be known as the Mother of Nations."

Then *Jigonhsasee* said: "I am a woman and do not make war. But the work I do is to feed the warriors passing my door on their way between east and west. They, too, must accept the New Mind or there will be no end to killing. Where wilt thou first take thy message?"

"I go toward the sunrise," replied *Deganawidah*.

"The direction thou takest is dangerous," said *Jigonhsasee*. "That way stands the house of a man who eats humans."

"That is the business I go about," said *Deganawidah*, "to bring such evils to an end so that all men may go about from place to place without fear."

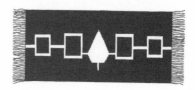

HIAWATHA SEES HIMSELF

WHEN DEGANAWIDAH came to the house of the "man who eats humans," he climbed to the roof and lay flat on his chest beside the smoke hole. There he waited until the man came home carrying a human body, which he put in his kettle on the fire. Deganawidah moved closer and looked straight down.

At that moment the man bent over the kettle. Seeing a face looking up at him, he was amazed. It was Deganawidah's face he saw reflected in the water, but the man thought it was his own. There was in it such wisdom and strength as he had never seen before nor ever dreamed that he possessed.

The man moved back into a corner of the house, and sat down and began to think.

"This is a most wonderful thing," he said. "Such a thing has never happened before as long as I have lived in this house. I did not know I was like that. It was a great man

42

who looked at me out of the kettle. I shall look again and make sure that what I have seen is true."

He went over to the kettle, and there again was the face of a great man looking up at him.

"It is true," he said. "It is my own face in which I see wisdom and righteousness and strength. But it is not the face of a man who eats humans. I see that it is not like me to do that."

He took the kettle out of the house and emptied it by the roots of an upturned tree.

"Now I have changed my habits," he said. "I no longer kill humans and eat their flesh. But that is not enough. The mind is more difficult to change. I cannot forget the suffering I have caused, and I am become miserable."

Then the man felt his loneliness and said, "Perhaps someone will come here, some stranger it may be, who will tell me what I must do to make amends for all the human beings I have made to suffer."

When he returned to the house, he met Deganawidah, who had climbed down from the roof, and they entered and sat down across the fire from each other.

"Today I have seen a strange thing," said the man. "I saw a face looking at me out of the kettle in this house where I live. It was my own face, but it was not the face of the man who has lived here. It was the face of a great man, but I am become miserable."

"Truly," said Deganawidah, "what has happened this

day makes a wonderful story. Thou hast changed the very pattern of thy life. The New Mind has come to thee, namely Righteousness and Health and Power. And thou art miserable because the New Mind does not live at ease with old memories. Heal thy memories by working to make justice prevail. Bring peace to those places where thou hast done injury to man. Thou shalt work with me in advancing the Good News of Peace and Power."

"That is a good message," said the man. "I take hold, I grasp it. Now what work is there for us both to do?"

"First, let us eat together," said Deganawidah. "I will go into the woods for our food. Do thou go to the stream and fetch water for the kettle. But be careful. Dip with the current. One must never go against the forces of nature."

When Deganawidah came back from the woods, he bore on his shoulders a deer with large antlers.

"It is on the flesh of the deer," said Deganawidah, "that the Holder of the Heavens meant men to feed themselves, and the deer's antlers shall be placed on their heads. Great men shall wear the antlers of authority, and by these emblems all men shall know those who administer the new order of Peace and Power which I am come to establish."

"What will this new order be called?" asked the man.

"When it is completed," replied Deganawidah, "it will be called by these names: Kanonsionni, the Longhouse, the League; and Kayanerenhkowa, the Great Peace, or the Great Law. Men shall live together in one community, as in the longhouse, and they shall live in peace because they live under one law."

Now not far from that place there lived a chief of the Onondagas named Atotárho,[*] who was a great wizard and evil. He was so cruel that he killed and devoured all men who approached him uninvited, and so strong that the birds flying over his lodge fell dead at his feet if he waved his arms. He had a twisted body and a twisted mind, and his hair was a mass of tangled snakes. No man liked to see him, and the sound of his voice carried terror through the land; but his power was mighty, and Deganawidah knew that the cause of peace could not be completed without him.

"Thou shalt visit this man Atotarho," said Deganawidah, "for he is of thy people, the Onondagas. He is ugly, but we need him. When he asks thee for thy message, say, 'It is Righteousness and Health, and when men take hold of it they will stop killing one another and live in peace.'

"He will not listen to thee, but drive thee away. Yet thou shalt come to him again and at last prevail. Thou shalt be called Hiawatha, He Who Combs, for thou shalt comb the snakes out of Atotarho's hair."

---

* Also known as Tadodaho (see Introduction). "Tadodaho" has survived as the title of the Chief of the Six Nations.

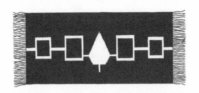

THE MOHAWKS
TAKE HOLD

BEFORE HE CONTINUED *his journey toward the sunrise, seeking the smoke of peoples, Deganawidah visited Atotarho to prepare his mind for Hiawatha's message. He found the wizard seated on a great rock in a glen.*

"I am come to prepare thy mind," said Deganawidah, "for the Good News of Peace and Power. When men accept it, they will stop killing, and bloodshed will cease from the land."

Atotarho's head was covered with snakes and his body was crooked. He loved disorder and hated peace, but he did not say so, for his mind was twisted and his workings were evil and indirect.

"When will this be?" he cried: "Hwe-do-né-e-e-e-eh?"

He drew out the last sound in a howl that carried far through the forest, striking fear into all who heard it. It was the mocking cry of the doubter who killed men by destroying their faith.

"It will be," replied Deganawidah. "I shall come again, with Hiawatha, who will comb the snakes out of thy hair."

Thence Deganawidah took his course toward the sunrise, toward the land of the Kanienga, the Flint Nation, or Mohawks. By the Lower Falls of the Mohawk River (Cohoes, New York), Deganawidah made camp, and in the evening sat beneath a tall tree and smoked his pipe.

A man of the Kanienga passing by saw him and asked, "Who art thou?"

"I am Deganawidah," he replied. "The Great Creator from whom we are all descended sent me to establish the Great Peace among you."

"There is no peace here," said the man. "But I will take thee to my village, and thou shalt explain this message to the people."

So Deganawidah presented the Good News of Peace and Power, of Reason and Law, to the Mohawks in that place, and the people were glad, for they found it a good message.

But their chiefs were cautious and held back.

The Chief Warrior said to Deganawidah, "Thou speakest well. Reason and law and peace are good things. But east and west of our village are powerful tribes who are always at war with us. Whence can peace come?"

"It will come," said Deganawidah, "with the Words of

the Law. The Great Binding Law—that is Peace."

Then said the Chief Warrior to the people, "What this man says is good, but is it true? Let him give us a sign. Let him climb to the top of a tall tree by the falls, and we shall cut it down over the cliff. If he lives to see the sunrise, we shall accept his message."

So all moved to the place where the tree stood beside the falls.

"If thou livest to see tomorrow's sunrise," said the Chief Warrior, "we shall take hold of thy message."

Deganawidah climbed the tree to the topmost branch. Then the Mohawks cut the tree down so that it fell over the cliff into the water. The people watched to see if Deganawidah came up, but there was no sign of him.

"Let us return at sunrise," said the Chief Warrior, and the people went back to their village for the night.

Next morning, before sunrise, a man of the Kanienga coming to the place by the falls where the tree had fallen, saw at a little distance across the cornfields a column of smoke rising, and going toward it he saw a man seated by his fire. It was Deganawidah.

When the man returned to the village and told what he had seen, the people came out and brought Deganawidah back to the place of council.

The Chief Warrior spoke. "Yesterday," he said, "I was in great doubt, for words, however good, do not always betoken the thing that is. Now I am in doubt no longer. This is a great man, who reveals to us the Mind of the Master of Life. Let us accept his message. Let us take hold of the Good News of Peace and Power."

Then said Deganawidah: "The day is early and young, and so also is the New Mind young and tender. And as the new sun rises and proceeds surely on its course in the sky, so also shall the Young Mind prevail and prosper among men. There shall be peace. Your children and your grandchildren and those whose faces are yet beneath the ground shall live under the sky without fear."

Thus the Mohawks were the first nation to take hold of the Great Peace. They were the founders of the League.

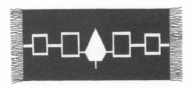

WORDS OF WAMPUM

MEANWHILE HIAWATHA HAD *met failure among the Onondagas. The people were with him; they accepted the New Mind and desired to take hold of the Peace. But Hiawatha could make no headway against their chief, Atotarho.*

Three times Hiawatha called a council. Three times the councilors set out to visit Atotarho and straighten his twisted mind. But three times the wizard's evil power rushed out to meet them. Three times their councils were dissolved. Some of the Onondagas, approaching Atotarho in their canoes, were drowned by the waves. Others were set fighting among themselves. Blood was shed. Hiawatha was not injured in his body, but he was wounded in his mind by the obstructions placed in his path.

One day he heard Atotarho's voice crying out of the air, "Hiawatha-a-a-a-a-a!" and he was troubled, for he knew that mischief was hatching.

Soon Hiawatha's three daughters were taken ill, one

after the other, and all died. Hiawatha's grief bowed him down.

"I shall be unable to perform the work of the Good Mind," he said, "because of this awful thing that has befallen me."

Seeing him thus depressed, the people came to comfort him, and they arranged a game of lacrosse to lift his mind. But when a mysterious bird dropped out of the sky, and the crowd, pursuing it, trampled his wife to death, his grief overcame him. He "split the sky" (struck south) and left the land of the Onondagas.

So began the journey that figures so prominently in Iroquois legend. Not far up among the mountains from Onondaga (Syracuse), Hiawatha came to the Tully Lakes, crossing one of them, it is said, with dry moccasins because the ducks at his request had lifted the water for him to pass.

Picking up shells from the lake bottom, he threaded them on three strings of jointed rushes as a mark of his grief. At night when he built his fire at that place, which he named Ohondogónwa, the Land of Rushes, he held the three strings in his hand and said:

"This would I do if I found anyone burdened with grief even as I am. I would take these shell strings in my hand and console them. The strings would become words and lift away the darkness with which they are covered. Holding these in my hand, my words would be true."

Every night when he made his fire, he set up two

crotched sticks, placed another across them, and from it he hung the three strings of shells. Then he sat down and repeated his saying:

"This would I do if I found anyone burdened with grief even as I am. I would take these shell strings in my hand and console them. The strings would become words and lift away the darkness with which they are covered. Holding these in my hand, my words would be true."

For many days Hiawatha was a wanderer, moving through the forest without direction, sometimes south and sometimes north and sometimes east.

"I can only rove about," he said, "since now I have cast myself away from my people."

When he came to settlements, the smoke from his fire at evening was seen at the wood's edge, but no one came to console him. Men knew that it was Hiawatha, for they had heard of his departure from Onondaga. They knew, too, that he was destined to go to the country of the Flint Nation; for a runner had come from the south, from a nation by the seashore, telling of a seer in that country who had dreamed that a man from the north should meet a man from the west in the country of the Kanienga, the Mohawks, and that together they should establish a Great Peace.

But no one took up the strings of wampum to condole with him.

He built himself a canoe and paddled down the Mohawk River till, on the twenty-third day after his departure from the Onondagas, he came to the village by the Lower Falls, and built his fire at the wood's edge.

That night Deganawidah went to the place where the smoke from Hiawatha's fire was seen rising.

As he approached, he heard the voice of Hiawatha, saying:

"This would I do if I found anyone burdened with grief even as I am. I would take these shell strings in my hand and condole with them. The strings would become words and lift away the darkness with which they are covered. Holding these in my hand, my words would be true."

Then Deganawidah came forward and, taking the strings from the horizontal pole and holding them, with others he had made, in his hand, he spoke, string by string, the several Words of the Requickening Address, used for all generations since in the Iroquois Condolence Ceremony.

"I wipe away the tears from thy face," said Deganawidah, "using the white fawn-skin of pity. . . . I make it daylight for thee. . . . I beautify the sky. Now shalt thou do thy thinking in peace when thine eyes rest on the sky, which the Perfector of our Faculties, the Master of All Things, intended should be a source of happiness to man."

Thus was Hiawatha's mind cleared of its grief.

"Now," said Deganawidah, "Reason has returned; thy judgment is firm again. Thou art ready to advance the

New Mind. Let us together make the laws of the Great Peace, which shall abolish war."

So when the Great Law was completed, and for each item a string or belt of wampum had been provided to enable them to remember it the more easily, Hiawatha and Deganawidah carried the Words of the Great Peace to the nations of the west: the Oneidas, Onondagas, Cayu-gas, and Senecas.

As they went, they sang the "Peace Hymn," the Hai! Hai!:

Hail! Hail! Hail!

To the Great Peace bring we greeting . . .

That song is still sung, modified by the nostalgia of later generations for the golden age of the League's birth, whenever the ancient ritual is invoked for the installation of chiefs in the Great Peace.

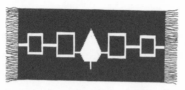

COMBING THE SNAKES
OUT OF ATOTARHO'S HAIR

ACCOMPANIED BY CHIEFS *of the Mohawk Nation, Deganawidah and Hiawatha first approached the Oneidas, the People of the Standing Stone, whom they had little difficulty in persuading to accept the Great Peace sponsored by their powerful neighbors, the Mohawks.*

Beyond the Oneidas lay the Onondagas, but the paralyzing cry of Atotarho, "Hwe-do-ne-e-e-e-eh? When will this be?" forced them to leave the Onondagas, the People of the Hills, and pass on to the Great Pipe People, the Cayugas.

The mild-mannered Cayugas, always quick to help their fellow humans, and a little fearful at their own situation between such powerful peoples as the Onondagas and Senecas, were glad enough to take hold of the Great Peace. So now, with three nations at their back, Deganawidah and Hiawatha returned to the politically minded Onondagas, and were able to convince their chiefs (all but Atotarho) that it would be well to join. Then, accompanied by the chiefs of four nations, Mohawks, Oneidas, Onondagas, and Cayugas, they carried the Peace Hymn to Canandaigua Lake, where they persuaded the two branches of the People of the Great Hill, the Senecas, warlike and independent though they were, to compose their rivalries and enter the Longhouse.

"Now," said Deganawidah, "we must seek the fire and look for the smoke of Atotarho. He alone stands across our path. His mind is twisted and there are seven crooks in his body. These must be straightened if the League is to endure."

So Deganawidah returned to Onondaga Lake and assembled the chiefs of five nations in the woods beside it.

"Come," said Deganawidah to Hiawatha, "thou and I alone shall go first to the Great Wizard. I shall sing the Peace Song and thou shalt explain the Words of the Law, holding the wampum in thy hand. If then we straighten his mind, the Longhouse will be completed and our work accomplished."

Accordingly, the two put their canoe into the lake and dipped their paddles.

As they neared the middle of the lake, they heard the voice of Atotarho, "Asonke-ne-e-e-e-e-eh? Is it not yet?"

"Truly," said Hiawatha, "the man is impatient."

The wind blew and the waves struck angrily against

60

the canoe as again they heard Atotarho's cry rush out to meet them: "Asonke-ne-e-e-e-eh! It is not yet!" But Deganawidah put his strength into his paddle, and in a few moments they beached their canoe at what is now known as Hiawatha Point, on the east shore of the lake, climbed the bank, and stood before the wizard.

"Behold!" said Hiawatha. "We two are come."

"Who are you?" demanded Atotarho.

"Hast thou not heard," responded Hiawatha, "of two who were to come to thee?"

"I have heard," answered Atotarho, "that Hiawatha and Deganawidah were on their way."

"Yea, truly," said Hiawatha, "and now we two are here."

"I have waited a long time impatiently."

"Thy impatience has caused our delay," said Hiawatha.

Then, holding the strings of lake wampum in his hand, he continued:

"These are the Words of the Great Law. On these Words we shall build the House of Peace, the Longhouse, with five fires that is yet one household. These are the Words of Righteousness and Health and Power."

"What is this foolishness about houses and righteousness and health?" said Atotarho.

Then Deganawidah spoke his message:

"The Words we bring constitute the New Mind, which is the will of Tarachiawagon, the Holder of the Heavens. There shall be Righteousness when men desire justice,

61

Health when men obey reason, Power when men accept the Great Law. These things shall be given form in the Longhouse, Kanonsionni, where five nations shall live in quiet as one family. At this very place, Atotarho, where the chiefs of five nations will assemble, I shall plant the Great Tree of Peace, and its roots shall extend to far places of the earth so that all mankind may have the shelter of the Great Law."

Atotarho said, "What is that to me?"

"Thou thyself," said Deganawidah, "shalt tend the Council Fire of the Five Nations, the Fire That Never Dies. And the smoke of that fire shall reach the sky and be seen of all men."

"Who shall bring this about?" asked Atotarho.

"Thou shalt, if thou desirest it. Thou shalt be the Head Chief of the Five Nations."

"Of course I desire this thing," said Atotarho, "if there be anything in it. But thou art a dreamer. Where is power to bring it to pass? Asonke-ne-e-e-e-e-eh! It is not yet!"

At that Hiawatha and Deganawidah returned as they had come across the lake to where the chiefs were waiting for them on the far shore.

"Make haste," said Deganawidah. "This is the time!"

They all put their canoes into the lake and paddled across. As they neared the middle, they heard the voice of Atotarho rush out to meet them, crying, "Asonke-ne-e-e-e-e-eh! It is not yet!" The wind lifted the waves against

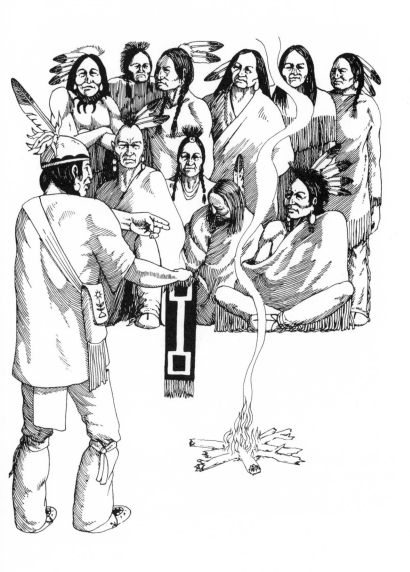

the canoes, but they put their strength into their paddles and, before the voice had died away, they stood before Atotarho.

"Behold!" said Deganawidah. "Here is Power. These are the Five Nations. Their strength is greater than thy strength. But their voice shall be thy voice when thou speakest in council, and all men shall hear thee. This shall be thy strength in future: the will of a united people."

Then the mind of Atotarho was made straight, and Hiawatha combed the snakes out of his hair.

Deganawidah laid his hand on Atotarho's body and said: "The work is finished. Thy mind is made straight; thy head is now combed; the seven crooks have been taken from thy body. Now thou, too, hast a New Mind. Thou shall henceforth preside over the Council, and thou shalt strive in all ways to make reason and the peaceful mind prevail. Thy voice shall be the voice of the Great Law. All men shall hear thee and find peace."

Then Deganawidah placed antlers on the heads of the chiefs in sign of their authority and gave them the Words of the Law.

UNITED NATIONS

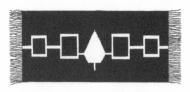

ANTLERS OF AUTHORITY

A S WE PASS FROM *legend to history with the story of that first Council by Onondaga Lake, at which Deganawidah presented the Five Nations with a constitution (which still lives), we naturally ask the question, "When did this happen?"*

The answer is not as simple and clear as we could wish it to be. The bringing together of the five separate parts of the League took, according to the legend, five days (i.e., five years). Actually, the Completed Longhouse had taken much longer in the building, decades or even generations. To set a precise date for the final consolidation of the Confederacy seems impossible. The Iroquois themselves say it happened "a long time ago"— "In the dark backward and abysm of time."

Chief William D. Loft once told me that when the first white man to question the Iroquois about the League asked, "When was this founded?" the Indians replied: "We can only tell you this way. The Kanonsionni *was already born* and working when you people first came to this country."

Some recent historians have set the approximate date at 1570. There is some evidence for that date, but it is by no means conclusive, and the spirit of the legends and ceremonies of the Iroquois must be set against it. The founding of the League is the central theme in Iroquois story and song and ritual, and that event is referred to today among the Indians as something of great antiquity. It was so spoken of during the nineteenth century in the work of the anthropologists Morgan and Hale, during the eighteenth century in the letters of Conrad Weiser, Pennsylvania's ambassador to Onondaga, and during the seventeenth century in the reports of the Jesuit missionaries. The League was called ancient in the earliest written records.

When Conrad Weiser in 1743 attended a meeting of the Onondaga Council, at which the founding of the League was rehearsed in song, he referred to the founders as "Ancient Chiefs." In 1691 Father Milet, a Jesuit missionary captured and adopted by the Five Nations, was given, as we read in the Jesuit Relations, the "ancient name" of one of "the first founders of the Iroquois republic," Otasseté, one who had been regarded "from all antiquity" (de toute ancienneté) as a mainstay of the nation. "From all antiquity" is surely too strong a term for a period of only 121 years (1570 to 1691). In 1654 another of the Jesuit Fathers noted that the League had been called the Longhouse or

Completed Cabin "from the earliest times" (de tout temps)—again too strong a term for a period, in this case, of only eighty-four years.

Horatio Hale, writing in 1881, expressed the opinion that the League had been founded about the middle of the fifteenth century. When in 1900 a committee of chiefs on the Six Nations Reserve wrote down the story of the founding of the League as it had been handed down to them, they set the date as far back as 1390.

In view of the air of antiquity which already hung over the League when it first came under the recorded observation of white men, it seems that an earlier date than 1570, possibly Hale's 1450 or thereabouts, may be taken as the approximate date of the founding.

* * * * *

The grass is still green on the meadow overlooking Hiawatha Point where Deganawidah placed antlers on the heads of the chiefs of the Five United Nations.

After investing them thus with the symbols of their authority, he gave them the Words of the Great Law. The speech which tradition ascribes to him on that occasion, preserved through the memory of successive generations of official Wampum Keepers, still stands as the constitution of the Five Nations.

"I am Deganawidah," it begins, in the Newhouse version

edited by Dr. Arthur C. Parker of the Rochester Museum, "and with the Five Nations' Confederate Lords I plant the Tree of the Great Peace. I plant it in your territory, Atotarho, and the Onondaga Nation, in the territory of you who are Firekeepers.

"I name the tree the Tree of the Great Long Leaves [i.e., the Great White Pine, according to Dr. William N. Fenton of the Smithsonian Institution]. Under the shade of this Tree of the Great Peace we spread the soft white feathery down of the globe thistle [the great White Mat of the Law, in Dr. Fenton's version] as seats for thee, Atotarho, and thy cousin Lords.

"We place thee upon those seats, spread soft with the feathery down of the globe thistle, there beneath the shade of the spreading branches of the Tree of Peace. There thou shalt sit and watch the Council Fire of the Confederacy of the Five Nations, and all the affairs of the Five Nations shall be transacted at this place before thee, Atotarho, and thy cousin Lords, by the Confederate Lords of the Five Nations."

The constitution of the Great Peace is not a defensive instrument dealing solely with safeguards against oppression and war. It is a positive thing, giving expression to the Five Nations' way of life.

"Our strength shall be in union," said Deganawidah, "and our way the way of reason, righteousness, and peace."

To begin with, it expresses the great principle of unity

in diversity, a principle that gave its peculiar strength to the Confederacy. Each separate nation, with its individual customs and local pride, knew that its chief assurance of essential independence lay in a union that guaranteed its way of life against all attack.

"The five Council Fires," said Deganawidah, "shall continue to burn as before and they are not quenched."

To the outside world the spirit of the League might seem to be expressed in the Latin motto E Pluribus Unum. But to the nations within the League its spirit might have seemed better expressed in the words Ex Uno Plura. The strength of the whole made safe the individual differences of the members.

If the Kanonsionni, the Longhouse, with its rafters of the Law, protected the five fires, it protected also the rights of the individuals who sat by them. The Iroquois cherished the Four Freedoms of our own day. Two of them received specific mention in the constitution: Freedom from Fear and Freedom from Want.

The avowed purpose of the union was to provide the strength that casts out fear.

"We bind ourselves together," said Deganawidah, "by taking hold of each other's hands so firmly and forming a circle so strong that if a tree should fall upon it, it could not shake nor break it, so that our people and grandchildren shall remain in the circle in security, peace, and happiness."

Freedom from Want was taken care of in the provision

that the hunting grounds should be open to all. There was to be common access to raw materials.

"We shall have one dish," said Deganawidah, "in which shall be placed one beaver's tail, and we shall all have a co-equal right to it, and there shall be no knife in it, for if there be a knife in it there will be danger that it might cut someone and blood would thereby be shed."

Freedom of Religion was regarded among the Five Nations as so natural a right as to require no mention in the constitution except in the case of adopted nations, to whom it was specifically granted. The religion of the Iroquois themselves, which was not unlike Wordsworth's modified pantheism, was practiced without hypocrisy or bigotry. Foreign peoples who joined them under the shelter of the Tree of Peace were allowed, and indeed encouraged, to worship in their own way. When in the eighteenth century the Iroquois adopted the tiny remnant of the Tutelo Nation, they saw to it that the beautiful religious observances of this Siouan people should be preserved. Dr. Frank G. Speck, in his remarkable study, The Tutelo Spirit Adoption Ceremony, shows how today the Cayugas, under whose wing the Tuteloes were taken some two hundred years ago, have assumed responsibility for this rite now that there are no longer any Tutelo-speaking people to attend to it for themselves.

Freedom of Speech was a right so deeply embedded in the Iroquois way of life as to need no attention in the constitution. Fires burning all over the Five Nations territory symbolized the right of public discussion. Besides the Great Council at Onondaga (the Fire That Never Dies), there were local fires in each nation, each clan, each family; and the women had their fires as well as the men.

There was one freedom that the Five Nations denied themselves: "Freedom, free to slay herself," the liberty to destroy their own liberties. They knew that great freedom demands, for its preservation, great self-restraint. Being aware how unscrupulous agitators used the right of free speech to spread diversive propaganda, they surrounded public debate with safeguards against that danger.

For one thing, the constitution provided that discussion in the Great Council should not be prolonged after nightfall. The physical conditions that foster frayed tempers and hasty judgments were thus avoided.

For another, the public discussion of an important proposition was not allowed to take place the same day it was received in Council. Time had to be allowed for study of the proposal. When, during that interval, it was seen that serious differences were likely to arise, these were aired in committee. The delegates of each nation discussed the proposal among themselves, compared their conclusions with those of other national groups, and, by tossing the ball back and forth in this manner, they arrived at compromises and accommodations likely to be satisfactory to all concerned. Public debate in the Great

Council did not, as a rule, begin until after this preparation; and so, each speaker having been previously instructed by his national delegation (the nation thus speaking "with one voice"), there were seldom heard any of those recriminations from popular leaders which are so apt to set the public by the ears.

There was no designated Bill of Rights, such as is provided in the first amendments to the American Constitution. The rights of man were so thoroughly entrenched in popular custom and everywhere taken so much for granted that any additional guarantees in the constitution seemed unnecessary. The constitution concerned itself less with rights than with duties. This is seen in the means taken to reconcile the principle of equal sovereignty with the facts of nature.

Certain members of the League were more powerful than others, and this fact was frankly recognized in the Longhouse and used to strengthen the structure. The Big Three—Mohawks, Onondagas, and Senecas, the "elder brothers"—were assigned determining roles in the administration of the League, especially in war and the conduct of foreign affairs. But the constitution found a way, by means of certain checks placed on them and by the balanced use of the veto, to see that none of the Big Three, nor all of them together, should abuse their power.

The Mohawks, a great military nation facing hostile Algonquin tribes to the east, were known as the Keepers of the Eastern Door of the Longhouse, and were accorded a Council veto. The Senecas, faced with vast multitudes of alien peoples on the west, were known as the Keepers of the Western Door, and, since they were numerically the strongest of all the Five Nations, it was fitting that they should supply, as they did, the two War Chiefs of the Confederacy. The Onondagas were the Fire Keepers or perpetual hosts. Their chiefs were also the permanent steering committee of the Great Council. They called meetings, prepared the agenda, and provided the chairman or moderator, Atotarho, who rendered decisions in case of disagreement among the other nations and who exercised the power of veto.

The Head Chief of the Onondagas, Atotarho, was Head Chief of the Five Nations, but his authority, and that of succeeding Atotarhoes, was closely circumscribed by the advice of his brother chiefs among the Onondagas and also by the checks embodied in the Council procedure as prescribed by the constitution.

Because of certain political exigencies at the time of the founding of the League, some nations had more representatives in the Great Council than others (the Onondagas had fourteen while the Mohawks had nine and the Senecas eight), but this was of no importance since, in the decisions of the Great Council, each nation spoke with only one voice and had only one vote.

Since each of the Five Nations retained its sovereignty,

77

it was necessary for the success of the League that its unity should be of the spirit and reside in the minds of all its citizens. To this end the constitution is filled with poetic symbols.

"We have now completed our power," said Deganawidah at the first Council by Onondaga Lake, "so that we, the Five Nations Confederacy, shall in future have only one body, one head, and one heart."

He gave them the symbol of the Tree, under the shelter of which the Five Nations gathered, and the symbol of the Fire around which they sat. He gave them as a further symbol the Bundle of Arrows, denoting strength through union.

Deganawidah took one arrow from each of the Five Nations and, tying the arrows together with deer sinews, said: "Now it is completed. I have made it tight. It will be impossible to bend it, and it will endure as long as there shall be generations. . . .

"I say to you it will not be right for one of the several nations to pull out its arrow."

The very name of the League, Kanonsionni, the Longhouse, was a symbol of unity. In the words of the Jesuit Relations, the name Kanonsionni signified that the Five Nations "constituted but one family."

Their symbols were not static but dynamic, looking forward to the growth and extension of the League. The Tree was growing, its Roots were extending, new Braces were being added (by the adoption of foreign peoples) to strengthen the walls of the Longhouse, and new Beams (amendments) were to be added to the Rafters of the Law. The spirit of progress and adventure united the five families gathered about their separate fires in the Longhouse. They were all crusaders for a better world.

Like Hiawatha they looked forward rather than back: looked forward to an ever-widening community in which the Law should enable reason and justice and peace to prevail, rather than back to the days of national jealousies and war.

As further symbols of an aggressive moral wholeness that should clear the mind of past evils and keep it clear, the Council ritual called for a great White Mat or Wampum Belt to be spread on the ground. White wampum signified purity or peace. A great Wing was provided to sweep from the White Wampum Belt any dust or dirt that might adhere to it (the dust and dirt signifying discord). A stick was laid at hand to be used when any creeping thing that might harm their grandchildren was seen approaching the White Wampum Belt. The stick was to remove tricky problems—the seeds of war—before they could reach the Council, set the chiefs at odds, and inflame the popular imagination.

"If you chiefs by the Council fire," said Deganawidah, "should be continually throwing ashes at one another, your people will go astray, their heads will roll, authority will be gone; your enemies then may see that your minds

79

are scattered, the League will be at a standstill, and the Good News of Peace and Power will be unable to proceed."

Special devices were inserted in the constitution to foster the spirit of union. The Great Council was itself such a device. Meeting not less than once a year, and being called by runners at short notice whenever important business arose, as when a special embassy from a foreign power arrived at Onondaga, the Council was kept constantly in the mind of the common citizen. All persons who cared to were encouraged to attend its meetings—much to the astonishment of the people of Pennsylvania when in 1736 chiefs of the Onondaga Council accompanied by scores of Indian followers sat down by a symbolic fire in the Great Meeting Place in Philadelphia to discuss affairs of state with Thomas Penn.

Meetings of the Great Council were a sight the Indians found well worth seeing. The chiefs in their buckskins (blankets, worn like Roman togas, were used after the white trader arrived on the scene), with coronets of feathers on their heads, sat about the fire in the Council house. The meeting was opened with prayer, as prescribed in the constitution, a prayer of thanksgiving to the Creator and to the various manifestations of his Mind in nature.

"Whenever the Confederate Lords shall assemble for the purpose of holding a council," Deganawidah had said, "the Onondaga Lords shall make an address and return thanks to the earth where men dwell, to the streams of water, the pools, the springs, and the lakes, to the maize and the fruits, to the medicinal herbs and trees, to the forest trees for their usefulness, to the animals that serve as food and give their pelts for clothing, to the great winds and the lesser winds, to the Thunderers, to the Sun, the mighty warrior, to the Moon, to the messengers of the Creator who reveal his wishes, and to the Great Creator who dwells in the heavens above, who gives all things useful to man, and who is the source and the ruler of health and life.

"Then shall the Onondaga Lords declare the Council open."

Songs were sung, commemorating the founding of the League; and the music of the beautifully intoned Jo-hah (U-huy, as Conrad Weiser described the sound), which circled the fire, the delegates of each nation repeating it in unison as a sign of approval, punctuated all the proceedings.

A colorful and dramatic touch was added by the use of wampum, the white and the purple (or "black"), the latter made from the purple spots in the clam shell. When a chief rose to address the Council, he held in his hand strings of wampum to show that his words were true. They served also as notes for both speaker and audience, helping the one to proceed with and the other to follow the steps in the argument. As each topic was disposed of, the speaker laid down a string of wampum, the strings being afterwards hung on a horizontal pole (such as Hiawatha had used) in the center of the Council house for all to see. The speaker who replied took these same strings from the pole and held them in his hand to refresh his memory as he reviewed, point by point, the preceding discourse.

Wampum was venerated among the Iroquois, tradition ascribing its first use to Hiawatha and Deganawidah. "Wampum is our heart," is an Indian saying recorded by Dr. Speck. Wampum gave words authority. Without wampum a message had no validity. To accept wampum was to accept the Word, the message it conveyed.

"They invariably observe this law," reported Father Jogues, a Jesuit missionary among the Mohawks who has since been canonized, "that whoever touches or accepts the present which is made to him is bound to fulfill what is asked of him through that present."

For important matters, such as treaties of peace, belts of wampum were prepared, often of considerable width, with designs inwrought by arrangement of the white and purple beads. Such treaty belts were preserved carefully, the explanation of each being memorized and handed down with the belt itself to succeeding Wampum Keepers, who were the national archivists.

All debate in Council was carried on quite literally "across the fire." The Mohawks and Senecas sat on the east side of the fire (the Mohawks north of the Senecas), while the Oneidas and Cayugas sat on the west side (the

Oneidas to the north). The Onondagas, as moderators, sat between the two groups, on the north side of the fire.

Propositions were discussed and conclusions arrived at through three separate stages of debate. First, each national delegation discussed the proposition and came to a conclusion so that it might speak with one voice. Second, the national unit compared its conclusions with that of its "brother" (the Mohawk with the Seneca, the Oneida with the Cayuga), in order that each side of the fire might speak with one voice. Then the Mohawks, as representing the Elder Nations, handed the joint decision of Mohawks and Senecas across the fire to the Oneidas, who received it on behalf of the Younger Nations. If the Younger Nations agreed, the matter was handed back across the fire to the Mohawks, who announced the agreement to the Onondagas, and the presiding officer, who inherited the title of "Atotarho," declared the matter settled. If, however, at any stage in this procedure a stubborn disagreement was encountered, the matter was returned for further study to the brotherhoods or to the national units, depending on the point in the line at which the break had occurred. If in the end no agreement could be found, the Mohawks announced this fact to the Onondagas, and they, through the voice of Atotarho, rendered a decision.

The names of the original chiefs, those said to have gathered at that first Council by Onondaga Lake, were passed down as titles and so served to strengthen the spirit of unity. The chiefs invested with these titles were living reminders of the story of the founding of the League. There was always a Hiawatha, an Atotarho, a Sharenkhówane, among them—though there was never again to be a Deganawidah, for "There shall be but one Deganawidah," said the father of his country, Deganawidah himself.

The song called "Hail!" (the Iroquois Hai! Hai!), which is also known as "The Six Songs" or the "Peace Hymn," served as a further bond of union. It was sung at the national ceremony of condolence and installation, held when a chief died and his successor was invested with the horns of office; but its tone was less one of lamentation than one of thanksgiving: thanksgiving to the League itself, the Great Peace, to their forefathers who had established it, to the men and women who preserved it, and (in the Onondaga version) to the children who should carry it on. Here is the Mohawk version:

THE PEACE HYMN
or Hai! Hai! (The Six Songs)

Hail! Hail! Hail!
Hail! Hail! Hail!
Once more we come to greet and thank the League;
Once more to greet and thank the nations' Peace.

84

Hai, hai, hai, hai, hai!
Hail, hail, hail, hail, hail!

Hail! Hail! Hail!
Once more we come to greet and thank the Kindred;
Once more to greet and thank the dead chief's
Kindred.
Hail, hail, hail, hail, hail!

Hail! Hail! Hail!
Once more we come to greet and thank the Warriors;
Once more to greet and thank the nations' Manhood.
Hail, hail, hail, hail, hail!

Hail! Hail! Hail!
Once more we come to greet and thank the Women;
Once more to greet and thank the mourning Women.
Hail, hail, hail, hail, hail!

Hail! Hail! Hail! that which our Forefathers accomplished!
Hail! Hail! Hail! the Law our Forefathers established!

O listen to us, listen, continue to hear us, our Grandsires!
O listen to us, listen, continue to hear us, our Grandsires!

In The Iroquois Book of Rites, *Horatio Hale, who calls*

these verses the National Hymn of the Iroquois and who suggests that "a comparison between it and other national hymns, whose chief characteristics are self-glorification and defiance, might afford room for some instructive inferences," prints a free translation in the metre of Longfellow's Hiawatha:

> To the great Peace bring we greeting!
> To the dead chief's kindred, greeting!
> To the warriors round him, greeting!
> To the mourning women, greeting!
> These our grandsires' words repeating,
> Graciously, O grandsires, hear us!

One of the constitution's best devices for knitting the nations together was the clan system. The relationship between members of a given clan was as binding as that between the members of a family. Yet these clans were intertribal. The three clans (in two phratries) that comprised the Mohawk Nation (1. Turtle; 2. Bear and Wolf) were the three clans (1. Wolf; 2. Turtle and Bear) that made up the Oneida Nation, and they were found as well in all the other nations of the Confederacy. The Onondagas, Cayugas, and Senecas had each a greater number of clans than the Mohawks (the Onondagas nine, the Senecas nine, and the Cayugas ten, including the three Bears: Big Bear, Younger Bear, and Suckling Bear), but these nations shared the Deer, Hawk, Heron, Eel, Sandpiper, and other clans among themselves.

Thus a man might travel from the Hudson to the Genesee and never lose touch with his kinsfolk. A Mohawk of the Turtle clan, making a journey to Canandaigua Lake in the Seneca country, would be entertained on the way by his Turtle kin among the Oneidas, Onondagas, Cayugas, and Senecas.

So strictly was this clan-family relationship observed that a man might not marry within his own clan. Our travelling Mohawk, while visiting his Turtle kin abroad, would have to be careful not to fall in love with a Turtle maiden, for he could not marry her. He could marry with Wolf or Bear, but never with Turtle. What's in a name? Nothing, so far as blood or biological law is concerned, but much, to the Iroquois mind, in the realm of the spirit. Intertribal clans meant international goodwill: the drawing together of distant peoples, not by vague phrases about human brotherhood, but by actual ties that touched the personal life.

Responsibility for cultivating the spirit of unity among the people was laid by Deganawidah squarely on the shoulders of the chiefs. By exhortation and example they were to show the way.

"It shall be the duty of all the Five Nations Confederate Lords," said Deganawidah, "from time to time as occasion demands, to act as mentors and spiritual guides of

87

their people and remind them of their Creator's will and words. They shall say:

" 'Hearken, that peace may continue unto future days!

" 'Always listen to the words of the Great Creator, for he has spoken. United people, let no evil find lodging in your minds.

" 'For the Great Creator has spoken and the cause of Peace shall not become old.

" 'The cause of peace shall not die if you remember the Great Creator.' "

If, however, the time ever came, said Deganawidah, that the Fire Dragon of Discord brought division into the Longhouse, and a high wind (war) uprooted the Tree of Peace, then the chiefs were to look for a Great Swamp Elm and, finding one "with large roots extending outward, bracing outward from the trunk," they with their people were to take shelter beneath it.

He instructed the chiefs to regard courage, patience, and honesty as the virtues most requisite to their responsibilities; and he urged them to think not so much of present advantage as of the future welfare of their people.

"When you administer the Law," he said, "your skins must be seven thumbs thick. Then the magic darts of your enemies will not penetrate, even if they prod you with their points.

"This is to be of strong mind, O chiefs: Carry no anger and hold no grudges. Think not forever of yourselves, O

*chiefs, nor of your own generation. Think of continuing
generations of our families, think of our grandchildren
and of those yet unborn, whose faces are coming from
beneath the ground."*

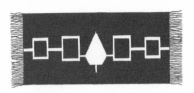

THE EAGLE
KEEPS WATCH

S OON ENOUGH AFTER *the founding of the League, the Eagle that Deganawidah had set on the Tree of Peace to spy out the approach of evil gave the alarm. The nations surrounding the Iroquois were not friendly. Their many Algonquin neighbors were actively hostile. Adjoining peoples of their own Iroquoian stock, who hemmed them in closely, were hardly less so. The Hurons especially, being far more numerous and in some ways better developed, treated the Five Nations with contempt and great cruelty. To the northeast, east, and south were hordes of Algonquin peoples, Montagnais, Agnakis, Mahicans, Delawares, and others, constantly at war with the upstart Confederacy.*

Everywhere the Five Nations were on the defensive. It was to be many years before, first, necessity, and then, success, developed among them the military tradition for which they have later been distinguished.

In the wars with the Adirondacks or Abnakis, whose raids from their strongholds in what is now northern New England had caused, in the opinion of Dr. Parker, the original coming together of the Five Nations, they were entirely successful. On the other hand, the long war with the Ojibways, who dwelt on the north and south shores of Lake Superior, was inconclusive. It ended in a treaty by which the two peoples agreed to live as brothers, but apart. In symbol of this treaty, whenever men of the Five Nations and Ojibways met, they exchanged a special sign of greeting, linking arms in the crook of the elbow. It is said on the Six Nations Reserve that this unusual greeting was reserved exclusively for the Ojibways, and was a mark of peculiar respect.

The Delawares to the south were subjected and given (symbolically) petticoats to wear. As "women" they were denied indulgence in the business of war.

The Mahicans, likewise, who in the late seventeenth century had managed to push the Mohawks far back from the Hudson, were finally defeated and reduced to the status of "nephew," which means "one under control like a package under the arm." Henceforth, like the Delawares, the Mahicans called the Iroquois "uncle."

To the north, meanwhile, there had arisen another and still more dangerous enemy. The French in Canada early in the seventeenth century had seen the spreading influence of the Iroquois, and they were resolved to chop the white roots of the Tree of Peace.

The Five Nations, on the other hand, for long preserved hopes that they might bring the French under the Tree.

"If you love, as you say you do, our souls, love our bodies also," they said, as recorded in the Jesuit Relations, "and let us be henceforth but one nation."

But the French, though they honestly desired to see the spread of Christ's gospel of peace throughout America, believed this could best be accomplished by the armies of their Most Christian King. From the days, there- fore, of Champlain, the founder of Quebec, they made lavish use of musket and cannon in the endeavor to brush the Five Nations, whom they found to be the chief obstacle to their advance on this continent, out of their way. The Jesuit missionaries, who have left a saga, in the Jesuit Relations, of devotion and heroism scarcely to be surpassed, were fiercely prejudiced against the Five Nations, having made their first contacts with Indians among the cruel and jealous enemies of the League. Some, indeed, of the missionaries deprecated the support their order gave the military in return for the clearance of Indian obstacles from the path of their missions. Others, however, approved of it, believing the Cross in America could best be carried forward on the musket barrel, and they expressed a desire for the extermination of the Five Nations. They saw, in the military prowess of the Iroquois, only blood lust and possession of the devil; in their peace talk, only lies and subterfuge; and in their restraint (as well attested by the records as are the cruelties which have made more popular reading), only stupidity.

For many years the Five Nations, under attack by the French, struck back, but not with their full power.

"It is a kind of miracle," wrote a French missionary, "that the Iroquois, although able to destroy us so easily, have not yet done so."

Unfortunately, this same missionary, who seems to have known (or understood) nothing about Deganawidah, thought the forbearance of the Iroquois sprang, not from policy, but from inadvertence; and he proposed that the French take advantage of this God-sent blindness, as he believed it to be, to destroy them.

Another missionary, marveling at the lofty ambition of the Five Nations, noted that "they think and say that their own destruction cannot occur without bringing in its train the downfall of the whole earth."

It was not, as the good Father supposed, the possession of firearms supplied by the Dutch that had put this lofty idea into Iroquois heads; it was the possession of the dream of world union under their Tree—under the shade, that is, of universal Law. They sincerely believed that unless the nations of the world sat down quietly under the Tree of Peace they would inevitably destroy themselves.

"They proclaim," wrote one of the Jesuit Fathers of a peace embassy the Iroquois proposed to send to Quebec

94

in the spring of 1664, "that they wish to unite all the nations of the earth and to hurl the hatchet so far into the depths of the earth that it shall never be seen in the future; that they wish to place an entirely new Sun in the Heavens, which shall never again be obscured by a single cloud; that they wish to level all the mountains, and remove all the falls from the rivers—in a word, that they wish peace. Moreover, as an evidence of the sincerity of their intentions, they declare that they are coming—women, and children, and old men—to deliver themselves into the hands of the French—not so much in the way of hostages for their good faith as to begin to make only one Earth and one Nation of themselves and us."

Unfortunately, the French and their Indian allies were not yet ready for Deganawidah's vision. When the Iroquois ambassadors, old and revered men, with their company of women and children bearing gifts of one hundred belts of wampum, some a foot wide, had set out on the long journey to Quebec, the Algonquins laid an ambush for them, killed some, captured others, and put the rest to flight.

"Thus the grand project of this embassy has vanished in smoke," concludes the narrative in the Jesuit Relations, "and instead of the peace which it was bringing us, we have on our hands a more cruel war than before."

The hostility of the French was based, in part, on economic grounds. The Hurons were a great trading nation, holding virtual control of the fur trade in the north and west. The French desired, by controlling the Hurons, to keep that trade for themselves. If the Five Nations succeeded in bringing the Hurons under the Great Tree—making of them "both but one people and only one land," as Father Jogues reported—the Iroquois would insist on sharing their trade. It will be recalled that freedom of trade, the sharing of hunting grounds, was one of the terms of the union.

So the French, using every weapon in the armory of power politics and secret diplomacy (their soldiers, governors, merchants, missionaries, ambassadors, and Indian allies were all agents of "the most Christian King"), persisted in thwarting the efforts of the Five Nations to extend their alliances to the north. The Hurons, at times, showed a desire for the alliance, but it always happened that their negotiations were blocked, or, if these were concluded, that the agreement itself was afterwards nullified. The Great White Roots extending to the north were constantly hacked at by secret enemies.

"Whenever a person or persons of other nations," Deganawidah had said, "shall cut or hack any of these four great roots [north, east, south, and west] which grow from the Great Tree we have planted ... then shall great trouble come into the seat of you Lords of the Confederacy."

By 1642 the Five Nations knew they were in great danger. The Hurons, secure in their numbers and the wealth the fur trade brought them, and comfortably assured of the support of the French and their circle of Indian allies, especially of the Andastes or Susquehannocks, whose armies and fortified towns (supplied with cannon) posed a deadly threat to the southern flank of the Iroquois, had become indifferent to peace with the Five Nations. The French, with the assistance of the Jesuit missionaries, were tying a noose about the Confederacy.

The constitution contained a provision for just such an emergency.

"Should a great calamity threaten the generations rising and living of the Five United Nations, then he who is able to climb to the top of the Tree of the Great Long Leaves [the Tree of Peace] may do so. When, then, he reaches the top of the Tree, he shall look about in all directions, and, should he see that evil things are indeed approaching, then shall he call to the people of the Five United Nations assembled beneath the Tree of the Great Long Leaves and say, 'A calamity threatens your happiness.'

"Then shall the Lords convene in council and discuss the impending evil."

The chiefs in council did discuss this evil, and it was decided to send north an embassy proposing peace to all the nations of those parts, French, Huron, Algonquin, and Montagnais.

Again the constitution gave directions:

"When the proposition to establish the Great Peace is made to a foreign nation, it shall be done in mutual council. The foreign nation is to be persuaded by reason and urged to come into the Great Peace."

Such a council was, accordingly, proposed and arranged for at Three Rivers on the St. Lawrence in Canada. Preparations were made by the Five Nations with great care, for they were resolved that the conference should be decisive, either for peace or war. It was so ordained in the constitution:

"When the Confederate Council of the Five Nations has for its object the establishment of the Great Peace among the people of an outside nation and that nation refuses to accept the Great Peace, then by such refusal they bring a declaration of war upon themselves from the Five Nations. Then shall the Five Nations seek to establish the Great Peace by a conquest of the rebellious nation."

The destinies of North America hung on the outcome of the conference at Three Rivers.

The Iroquois ambassadors were well supported. Some five hundred warriors accompanied the delegation and erected fortifications on the south shore of the St. Lawrence—again with faithful adherence to the words of the constitution:

"When the Lords of the Five Nations propose to meet in conference with a foreign nation with proposals for an acceptance of the Great Peace, a large body of warriors shall conceal themselves in a secure place safe from the

espionage of the foreign nation but as near at hand as possible."

Three canoes were sent across the river to meet the French, once more in such close compliance with instructions in the constitution as to show how firmly the Great Law was implanted in the minds of those who wore the antlers at Onondaga.

"Two warriors shall accompany the Union Lord who carries the proposals, and these warriors shall be especially cunning. Should the Lord be attacked, these warriors shall hasten back to the army of warriors with the news of the calamity which befell by the treachery of the foreign nation."

The remainder of the story may best be told in the words of the Jesuit Relations. The missionary Le Jeune described the incident faithfully, without, however, in the least understanding it, since he and the rest of the French, misled by an Indian informer (one of the Montagnais, who lived north and west of Three Rivers in the Saguenay region), allowed themselves to see nothing but treachery in the words and acts of Deganawidah's followers.

The three canoes "moved up and down before the fort, within hearing," writes Le Jeune; "one of the oldest men belonging to this squadron cried with a loud voice, speaking to the Savages: 'Listen to me! I come to treat for peace with all the Nations of these parts, with the Montagnais, with the Algonquins, with the Hurons; the land shall be

101

beautiful, the river shall have no more waves, one may go everywhere without fear.'"

No generous nor even adequate response to this appeal was forthcoming, though it had been made in the spirit, and almost in the words, of Deganawidah. Instead, an Algonquin Indian came out on the bank and called the Iroquois sachem a liar.

The Governor of New France, Monsieur the Chevalier de Montmagny (i.e., Big Mountain, which in the Iroquois tongue is Onóntio—a name the Indians gave to all succeeding governors of New France), now appeared on the scene and, being averse to risking his person among those whom he deemed savages, dispatched delegates to a conference which was to be held on the Iroquois side of the river.

The French delegates found themselves received in full council, the Indians sitting in a circle about a symbolic fire as the constitution prescribed. For the second time peace was proposed by the Five Nations.

Onágan, a chief, speaking with great earnestness and dignity, though not without a touch of the humor that so often warms Iroquois rhetoric, sent the Governor renewed proposals for a peace that should be all-embracing.

Taking "the hands of Father Ragueneau and of the Sieur Nicolet, the delegates to negotiate peace," writes Le Jeune, "then touching them on the face and on the chin, he said to them, 'Not only shall our customs be your customs, but we shall be so closely united that our chins shall be reclothed with hair, and with beards like yours.'"

The Governor, having delayed his reply considerably beyond the time agreed on, at length approached the south bank with several shallops filled with armed men; but he declined to go ashore. The Iroquois, accordingly, sent out a canoe containing three chiefs, who, presenting belts of wampum to show that their words were true, proposed for a third time a peace which should include the French and their Indian allies.

The Governor, haughty and insulting, hedged in his reply and, believing that the Iroquois offers were motivated solely by a fear of French arms, ventured a show of force.

Whereupon the Iroquois raised above their fortification on the bank an Algonquin scalp as a declaration of war, and proceeded to make their own show of force in a manner to cause Montmagny mountains of astonish-ment. Portaging their canoes to avoid a trap the Governor had laid for them with his armed vessels, and retiring to the shelter of stronger and better-manned fortifications in the woods than the French had dreamed of, they proceeded to work for peace by methods they were assured the white man would understand better than he understood the etiquette of Deganawidah's peace council.

"Thus," concludes Le Jeune, "the war with these tribes has broken out more fiercely than ever."

The Iroquois gave a good account of themselves.

"It is therefore a marvel," we read elsewhere in the Jesuit Relations, "that so few people work such great havoc and render themselves so redoubtable to so large a number of tribes. . . ."

Throughout the proceedings at Three Rivers in 1642, even in their military dispositions, the Five Nations had followed both the spirit and the letter of Deganawidah's constitution, their guide to international law. That same law had taught them that war and conquest were never to be regarded as ends in themselves. The Five Nations, accordingly, did not give up hope of ultimate peace with the French. Three years after the Three Rivers fiasco, the war in the meantime not having been pushed to the extreme of which they were capable, the Five Nations tried again for peace.

At Three Rivers in 1645, the Mohawk chief, Kiotsaeton, made another appeal in the spirit of Deganawidah. In a moving address he referred to passing, as he came north for the conference, "the place where the Algonquins massacred us last Spring. . . . I turned away my eyes for fear of exciting my anger," he continued; "then, striking the earth and listening, I heard the voice of my Forefathers massacred by the Algonquins. When they saw that my heart was capable of seeking revenge, they called out to me in a loving voice: 'My grandson, my grandson, be good; do not get angry. Think no longer of us for there is no means of withdrawing us from death. Think of the living—that is of importance; save those who still live from the sword and fire that pursue them; one living man is better than many dead ones.' After having heard those voices I passed on, and I came to you, to deliver those whom you still hold."

Kiotsaeton asked for the return of prisoners, presented wampum to clear the river of waves, and invited the French and their allies to join them in a peace that should be cemented by trade. His mission was successful.

But the peace concluded was not a lasting one. The Hurons who were included in it, continued to keep their trade to themselves. Next year, 1646, the whole Huron fur fleet went to Montreal, and the furs they could not sell there (for lack of goods among the French inhabitants sufficient to buy such quantities of pelts) went back to the Huron country. Observing that, the Iroquois understood that to the Hurons peace meant no more than an armistice, a cessation of fighting, and not the brotherliness and good sense of Deganawidah's vision. To the Five Nations, peace and trade were inseparable.

When in 1647 the Five Nations learned further that the Hurons had made an aggressive alliance with the Susquehannocks, who promised to "lift the axe" whenever the Hurons called on them to do so, they knew there was only one way. Delenda est Carthago: the Hurons must be destroyed.

Of what happened to that unhappy people, once the Five Nations had made up their minds, the Jesuit Relations bear mournful witness. In 1649 the Hurons ceased to exist as a nation.

The real enemy was still France, and the Five Nations proceeded to weaken her further by depriving her of the more powerful of her remaining Indian allies. They marked the whole Huron circle for extinction. In a series of campaigns which is one of the near miracles of North American military history, they put out of business the Tobacco Nation, the Neutrals, the Eries, and finally, in 1675, the mighty Susquehannocks.

These people were all defeated and dispersed, some fleeing to far nations for refuge and others coming in, as the Five Nations had always hoped they would do, to receive welcome and shelter under the Tree of Peace. These latter were adopted, and formed thereafter strong props to the Longhouse.

Whole villages of Hurons reestablished themselves comfortably in the Seneca country, where the Jesuit missionaries soon after found them and renewed acquaintanceship with old friends from the Georgian Bay region. A remnant of the Susquehannocks, adopted by the Oneidas, became so thoroughly at home among them that they gave up their own language and spoke Oneida. Yet they never altogether lost their national identity. Many years later they were sent back to their old territory in the Susquehanna Valley, establishing themselves at Conestoga, near Lancaster, Pennsylvania, where they remained till the Paxton Boys, a band of frontier ruffians from the neighborhood of today's Harrisburg, wiped them out in the massacres of 1763.

Those were the great days of Iroquois military history. The Five Nations had shown that a disposition to peace need not breed softness, and that Peace armed with Power and guided by Reason is irresistible. In less than thirty years they had broken the ring forged around them. Guided by the Eagle That Sees Afar, they had invaded Canada, defied the power of France, and destroyed her Indian allies. They were now the guardians of the peace throughout the woods of eastern North America. Their Tree stood firm, and, as they said, "spread its roots to a vast distance."

When the French, following Denonville's expedition of 1687 from across Lake Ontario against the Senecas, claimed title to the Iroquois country, the Five Nations made a neat reply. They admitted that the French had formerly come to the Mohawk country, as they had more recently come to the Seneca country, where they had burnt some bark houses and cut down the corn; but, they added, "if that be a good title, then we can claim all Canada."

WORLD CITIZENS

I N EXPLAINING THE GOOD NEWS *to a chief named Degaihógen, Deganawidah presented a vision of a world community.*

"What shall we be like," Degaihogen had asked, "when this Reason and Righteousness and Justice and Health have come?"

"In truth," replied Deganawidah, "Reason brings Righteousness, and Reason is a power that works among all minds alike. When once Reason is established, all the minds of all mankind will be in a state of Health and Peace. It will be as if there were but a single person."

When the Longhouse with five fires had been erected and the Tree of Peace planted at Onondaga, Deganawidah's mind leaped forward to the next great adventure: the union, under the shelter of the Tree, of all the nations of mankind. Hiawatha, instructed by Deganawidah, had announced wherever he went on his early mission that the purpose of the Good News was to make peace and contentment "prevail among the peoples of the whole earth." Now, at the first council, Deganawidah informed the chiefs that the Tree of Peace had sent forth roots in all directions, the Great White Roots of Peace.

"These roots," he said, "will continue to grow, advancing the Good Mind and Righteousness and Peace, moving into territories of peoples scattered far through the forest. And when a nation, guided by the Great White Roots, shall approach the Tree, you shall welcome her here and take her by the arm and seat her in the place of Council. She will add a brace or leaning pole to the Longhouse and will thus strengthen the edifice of Reason and Peace."

Throughout their history the Five Nations have sought to add such braces to the Longhouse: the Tuscaroras of Iroquoian stock from North Carolina, the Nanticokes of Algonquin stock from Maryland's Eastern Shore, and the Tuteloes of Siouan stock from Virginia, by the methods of peace; Hurons, Neutrals, Eries (all of their own stock), and many others, by the methods of war. Foreign nations which, of their own accord, sought shelter under the Tree were given a generous welcome.

The adoption of the Tuscaroras, "on the cradle-board," was not an unmixed blessing to the Five Nations, who found these newcomers not only populous but also a somewhat obstreperous people.

"A long time ago," said a Seneca councillor to Dr. Fen

ton, "the Tuscaroras came to us and asked to stop over-night. We took the Tuscaroras under our wing, and now they live to itch us like fleas."

Yet, having once accepted them, the Five Nations did not thrust them out. Indeed, they renamed the League the Six Nations when they were adopted, and today the Tuscaroras are an influential part of the Six Nations in western New York as well as in Canada. The "cradle-board" reservation was only a technicality. The Tuscaroras sat in council and spoke their mind, though through the lips (symbolically) of the nation that sponsored them. In like manner the Nanticokes ("who first founded witchcraft"), the Tuteloes, and the Delawares, when they sat down under the Tree, were allowed to use the voice of the Cayugas, their sponsors, to express their thoughts in the Great Council, their representatives being given seats on the Cayuga side of the fire.

The constitution of the Confederacy provided rules for the adoption of foreign peoples and also for their expulsion if they should attempt in any way to weaken the League. There were rules for inviting nations to enter the Peace, and further rules for making war on them should they decline the invitation.

Even the War Song to be used in extending the Great Peace by force of arms finds a place in that section of the constitution called the Laws of War and Peace:

> *... I am of the Five Nations*
> *And I shall make supplication*
> *To the Almighty Creator.*
> *He has furnished this army.*
> *My warriors shall be mighty*
> *In the strength of the Creator...*
> *For it was he who gave the song,*
> *This war song that I sing!*

Dr. Parker recalls that, when the Eries asked by what power the Five Nations demanded their surrender, the Iroquois replied, "The Master of Life fights for us."

* * * * *

When the first council of the United Nations ended, Deganawidah gave the chiefs a farewell in words of both warning and hope.

"If men should ever become indifferent to the League," he said, "perhaps I may stand here again among your descendants. If the Great Peace should fail, call on my name in the bushes, and I will return.

"Now my work is finished. I shall cover my body with bark and bury myself in the ground. There I shall hear how men tend the Longhouse I constructed for them here on the earth.

"These are the number of my words."

With that the man Deganawidah vanishes from sight. Neither history nor legend tells us how, when, or where he died. But we know that, even after he had covered his body with bark and returned to his mother, the Earth, no blood flowed from the sentinel tree at the settlement where he was born. His mission was successful. His work stands.

TO AMERICA'S OLDEST ALLY
THE IROQUOIS CONFEDERACY
"PEOPLE OF THE LONG HOUSE"

MOHAWKS, ONEIDAS, ONONDAGAS, CAYUGAS,
SENECAS – TO WHOM WERE LATER ADDED
THE TUSCARORAS CONSTITUTING

THE SIX NATIONS

FOUNDED BY DEGANAWIDAH AND HIAWATHA WHO PLANTED THE
TREE OF PEACE AT ONONDAGA (SYRACUSE) SOMETIME BEFORE THE
COMING OF COLUMBUS.

THEY EXCELLED IN STATESMANSHIP AND THE ART OF DIPLO-
MACY. AFTER THE WHITE MAN CAME, DURING MORE THAN A
CENTURY OF INTERCOLONIAL STRIFE, THEY LOYALLY PROTECTED
THE INFANT ENGLISH COLONIES, SHOWED THEM THE WAY TO
UNION, AND SO HELPED PREPARE THE AMERICAN AND CANADIAN
PEOPLE FOR NATIONHOOD.

IN MEMORY OF OUR BELOVED BROTHER
TO-RI-WA-WA-KON (DR. PAUL A. WALLACE)
WHO, THROUGH HIS WRITINGS, SHOWED THE IROQUOIS
CONFEDERACY AS IT TRULY EXISTED. THANK YOU,
TORIWAWAKON, FOR YOUR GREAT WORK.

Monument to Paul Wallace

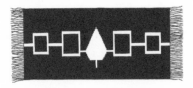

EPILOGUE

P AUL A. W. WALLACE'S White Roots of Peace, although brilliantly insightful in its rendition of elements of Haudenosaunee (or Iroquois) culture during the seventeenth century, did not have the benefit of important material relating to more recent times. As Wallace was researching the book, clouds were gathering that would bring five decades and more of intensified conflict for the People of the Longhouse. Some of the most severe threats to the existence of the League were forming as Wallace was writing.

Today the Iroquois occupy fifteen communities which stretch from southwestern Quebec to Oklahoma. Since the time of the American Revolution, the United States and Great Britain (and her successor state, Canada) have adopted the position that the League was dissolved during the revolution. These non-Indian governments have refused to give recognition to the collective sovereignty of the Confederacy, even though a number of these communities have continued to send delegates to Onondaga and carry on the political culture of the Great League.

Since about 1721, when the Tuscarora joined the League, the Confederacy has been composed of six sovereign Indian nations, each linked to the other through clanship ties, custom, and tradition: the Mohawk, Oneida, Tuscarora, Onondaga, Cayuga, and Seneca. During the nineteenth century, the peoples on the Grand River Six Nations Reserve near Brantford, Ontario, conducted meetings to manage the affairs which arose in their territories. The Six Nations Council, which is convened at Onondaga near Syracuse, New York, continues to function as the center of most of the meetings of the whole League, and today chiefs of the Grand River Country attend meetings at Onondaga and vice versa.

The Iroquois are one of the largest groups of Indians in North America, but they are no longer as unified as they once were. Around 1666, as a result of military pressure from New France, a significant number of Mohawk from the Mohawk Valley town of Kahnawake moved to the St. Lawrence Valley. Although they maintained kinship ties and informal political connections, the St. Lawrence Valley Mohawk operated independently and sometimes at odds with the League. In 1687, for example, Mohawk warriors acted as scouts for the military invasion of Iroquoia directed by New France's Governor Denonville. Even though such ruptures took place, St. Lawrence Valley Mohawk often attended meetings of the League. Although their participation was largely informal, it sometimes proved to be critical.

The League was incredibly elastic. During the so-called Beaver Wars, when France and (for the most part) England competed for economic hegemony in the northeast woodlands, Iroquois villages were sometimes known to disagree with the decisions of the League council concerning issues of trade and even sometimes issues of peace and war. The resulting shifting alliances stimulated intensive diplomacy, much of which took place at Onondaga or at the behest of the officers of the League. Some historians have seen these shifting alliances and uneven exercises of economic interest as signs of weakness of the League, but the Confederacy Council functioned as a diplomatic vortex during times of trouble as well as times of peace. Although the League could command respect but could not demand obedience, its continued survival through periods of disastrous violence attests to its strength, not its weakness. The British colonies, it can be pointed out, suffered from similar problems of mutual hostility, renegade governors, and militias that took provocative actions with the potential to start wars.

The two most significant crises for the League were the Seven Years' War and the American Revolution. The result of the Seven Years' War was that France was expelled from North America as a significant economic and military power. This had the effect of shifting a balance of power that had been in place for over a century. The groups contesting for North America before that war were France, England, the Anglo-American colonists, the French colonists, and the various Indians. Following the war, the French-speaking colonists and France were, at least for the time, removed as significant forces. This meant that Indian leverage, including that of the Haudenosaunee and its allies, was considerably reduced. One of the results was that English colonists began almost immediately to become more aggressive in their efforts to gain Indian territory, and the British Crown was moved to blunt their efforts with promises to the Indians that Indian territory would be protected.

By the time of the American Revolution, significant changes were in the wind in the Indian country. The country of the People of the Longhouse was, in 1775, no longer divided into distinct territories. There were, at that time, Indian towns with mixed Indian populations (Indians of different cultural origins living in the same town). Bostonian missionaries had taken an interest in the Indians. Just as French Jesuits had penetrated the Mohawk country a century earlier, the Reverend Samuel Kirkland found converts among the Oneida during the decade prior to the revolution. Some Oneida warriors organized to challenge the power of the Confederacy chiefs, converting to Kirkland's brand of New England puritanism and acting in peculiarly individualistic ways. Several years before the revolution broke out, Oneida "warriors" had already joined the Tryon County militia, the frontier military organization that would lead the rebel challenge to British occupation of what was then the frontier in New York.

The British representative in the Indian country was their Indian agent, Sir William Johnson. Sir William had spent a lifetime of service to the Crown among the Indians, had sired several children among them, and was trusted by many of them. Some of his Mohawk relatives were extremely loyal, including Joseph Brant, brother of John-son's Indian wife, Mary (or Molly) Brant. Before the hostilities between the American colonists and Britain broke out, these Mohawk and Oneida Iroquois were committed to polar interests that many of the other members of the League felt were contradictory to the interests of the League.

When hostilities broke out, the Grand Council resisted pressure from both sides to join in the violence. The Onondaga were especially dedicated to a course of neutrality, as were significant leaders among the Seneca. The Mohawk Valley Mohawk, especially Joseph Brant, were determined to align their fortunes with the British. Many Oneida of the Oneida "warrior" faction were already committed to the American cause. At a critical moment during the war, while the League was being courted by both sides, disaster struck Onondaga in the form of a plague that killed some ninety people, including many of the Onondaga chiefs. The Onondaga sent messages to their allies that they could not host meetings of the League at that time.

In the absence of Confederacy policy, the various factions of warriors, in meetings with their non-Indian friends, took matters in their own hands. The British, determined to crush the Americans in a devastating offensive on Fort Stanwix, called meetings with the warriors and pleaded and cajoled them to join their effort. Confident of victory over practically untrained American militia, they offered to allow the Indians to be spectators while they chastised the Americans. A considerable body of Indians followed the British army to American-held Fort Stanwix. The British military commanders, however, proved to be remarkably unprepared. The attacking army moved slowly, allowing defenders to prepare the fort. The British failed to bring the artillery necessary to breach the walls and, while the British army settled in, Americans sent General Herkimer with a column to break the siege.

The Tryon County militia called up its reserves, including its Oneida and Tuscarora enlistees, and marched toward the fort. The British at Stanwix sent some of their soldiers and a large contingent of Indians to meet the relief column. They met at Oriskany in a bloody battle during which Oneida warriors fought valiantly on the American side, and Iroquois warriors, mainly Seneca, took the brunt of the fighting on the other. The Americans suffered serious casualties and were forced from the field, their commander mortally wounded, and a number of Oneida and Tuscarora warriors fighting on the American side were killed and injured.

The battle at Oriskany was a kind of turning point. Although the League had not declared war, and although League policy was one of neutrality, Iroquois warriors were by custom free to enlist themselves as mercenaries in the cause of their choice as long as they did not rupture the League itself. The Americans interpreted Indian participation in the fighting as indicating that the Confederacy had entered the war on the side of Britain, and they were able to survive long enough to frustrate the British war effort and to win the war. When Britain capitulated in 1783, the British negotiators of the peace failed to make provisions for the fair and equitable treatment of her Indian allies, including the Iroquois. This meant that the Indians whose warriors had fought on the side of Britain were left substantially to the mercy of their enemies. It was a failure that would not be easily forgotten.

Although they had been treated disgracefully by their British allies, a large contingent of Iroquois followed Joseph Brant to Canada after the war. The British, for their part, did try to find a new country for their Iroquois allies along the Grand River. Other lands were made available at Theyendenaga. A significant number of Iroquois remained in New York. Except for the Oneida and Tuscarora, those who remained in New York were now the neighbors of bitter enemies who had designs on Iroquois lands.

New York State was a particularly aggressive player in the matter of Indian lands. Under the Articles of Confederation, New York moved to gain claim to title to Indian lands as soon as it could. Land frauds and violence to Indians by frontiersmen were so common and so disrupting that in 1790 Seneca chief Cornplanter informed U.S. president George Washington that unless something was done to address these injustices the Iroquois were prepared to launch into one last war with the United States and then to flee to Canada rather than see their lands quietly taken through fraud and coercion. At the time, the president was busy with other wars on the Indian front, and the United States was nearly bankrupt. Washington, who had early in his career taken an anti-Indian position, came to adopt the view that Indians should be treated honorably by the United States. He is, in this regard, practically the only American president to take this view and act on it. In 1790 he obtained passage of an act of Congress, the 1790 Non-Intercourse Act, whereby the U.S. government guaranteed to the Indians that the United States would see that no fraud clouded land transfers involving the states.

New York State promptly adopted a policy of ignoring the 1790 Non-Intercourse Act and moved aggressively to obtain as much Iroquois land as possible. A cornerstone of this policy, and one in which the U.S. government collaborated, was to ignore the existence of the collective rights of the League and to treat each of the Iroquois nations individually. Although there is no question that the League reorganized following the American Revolution, and no question that there were powerful cultural revitalizations, including the rebuilding of the Iroquois religion following the visions of Seneca prophet Handsome Lake, it became the political policy of New York State to ignore the existence of the League and its political rights.

One of the results was a series of land swindles and takings from 1784 to 1842 during which the Iroquois in New York lost possession of over 95 percent of their country. During this period some of the Oneida, the loyal allies of the Americans, lost almost all their lands in New York. The majority of that nation found new homes in a small community near present-day St. Thomas, Ontario, and a much larger community near present-day Green Bay, Wisconsin. The Wisconsin Oneida eventually lost almost all of their new lands through federal allotment acts that essentially took the land from the Oneida Nation by legislative fiat.

The Cayuga Indians lost most of their lands in New York State through fraudulent treaties, and most of them moved to reservations in the Oklahoma Territory and to the Grand River Country, though some have taken up residence among the Seneca at Cattaraugus and Allegany. The Onondaga lost most of their land in state treaties made prior to 1800. The Mohawk lands in New York were ceded by treaties signed, not by the Mohawk Nation or the Six Nations, but by two individuals—John Deserontion and Joseph Brant—in 1797. Most of the Seneca lands were lost through a series of purchases by private individuals and companies, including John Morris, one of the financiers of the revolution.

The threats to Haudenosaunee's continued existence, which were gathering as Paul A. W. Wallace was writing White Roots of Peace, had their origins in the Seneca country well over a century earlier. Since 1810 David Ogden and his (and his partners') heirs in the guise of the Ogden Land Company had acquired the interests of the Holland Land Company and pursued an aggressive policy of obtaining Seneca land through whatever means possible, including bribery, coercion, and outright fraud. Their efforts culminated in a treaty presented to Congress in 1838, which would have resulted in the removal of the remaining Iroquois in New York State to lands in Oklahoma Territory. Quakers and other friends of the Seneca joined with a great majority of the Seneca people in denouncing the treaty as fraudulent. Upon subsequent examination, even Congress determined that the treaty had not lived up to the very minimal standards accorded to Indian treaty making during this period because of evidence of extensive forgery, bribery, and coercion. A new treaty was fashioned, the so-called Compromise Treaty of 1842, which returned two of four Seneca reservations: Cattaraugus and Allegany. Two other reservations, Buffalo Creek and Tonawanda Creek, were lost to the Seneca during the exchange. The Tonawanda Seneca, who never signed any treaty relinquishing their lands, refused to leave and remained as "squatters" on the land swindled from them until they were allowed to "purchase" some of it back in 1867.

A careful reading of the history of the 1838 treaty will reveal that it replicated a pattern by then familiar in Indian affairs. It developed through a combination of Christian proselytization and the political clout of wealthy land speculators. Some of the Seneca chiefs, who had joined what was then called the Christian party, apparently came to believe strongly that their pagan (non-Christian) brethren would be best served were they to remove to an Indian country far away. Some of these individuals were rewarded for their participation in this way of thinking with what amounted to bribes and promises that when the others left, they would be allowed to remain and keep possession of their homes.

During these same years the Allegany Reservation, at 30,000 acres, was the largest of the Iroquois holdings remaining in New York. The Allegany River valley offered *a tempting route for the Erie Railroad. Shortly after the railroad appeared, white farmers, merchants, and railroad workers began occupying land at Carrollton and at what would later be designated the city of Salamanca. These lands were at first leased from individuals and later by the Seneca Nation at very low rates, but as the towns developed, conflicts arose around renewal of rentals.*

In 1848 a "revolution" occurred in the Seneca country. Angered in part by the past history of corruption (almost exclusively among the Christian chiefs), a group of "reformers" moved to gain recognition of a new form of government. The vote to determine whether the Seneca wanted the new "elected" form of government or to keep a version of the traditional government was framed in a referendum that asked people whether the government should receive the monies due the nation or if these monies should be divided among the people in per capita payments. Per capita payments won, and the traditional form of government was replaced among the Seneca at Cattaraugus and Allegany with an election form of government similar to that conducted in New York's municipalities. Per capita payments were soon suspended.

One of the proposed advantages of the new Seneca government that had been urged by the "reformers" was an assurance that the new government would be more amenable to leasing the lands used by the railroad and its service businesses at what would become Salamanca.

The U.S. government seized the opportunity, and upon federal recognition the Seneca Republic was born. This new form of government signaled a rift with the League, which did not recognize "elected" leaders. Seneca representation at League meetings shifted to the Tonawanda Seneca, while delegates from Cattaraugus and Allegany attended League functions less and less frequently. The Tonawanda Seneca, meanwhile, had refused to move from their lands, which had been ceded by the Treaty of 1838 and had not been returned in the Treaty of 1842. They would live in a state of uncertainty until they finally regained title to a small portion of their former lands in 1867.

Meanwhile, Salamanca grew rapidly. The Allegany Reservation was a valuable property, one which even contained some oil and gas reserves. In time, Salamanca became a small city, and by 1875 it could muster votes in Congress to create congressionally enacted leases under which white settlers could occupy Seneca lands at bargain rentals. By 1888 politicians in Salamanca and the surrounding county were actively pursuing ways to obtain outright ownership of Salamanca and the related "Congressional villages." These politicians dominated a New York Assembly committee which issued "Assembly Document 51—Report of the Special Committee Appointed by the Assembly of 1888 to Investigate the 'Indian Problem' of the State," a document proclaiming that the solution to the "Indian problem" was the dissolution of the *political existence of the Indians. At least some of these politicians were operating under what can be described as conflicts of interest because they owned businesses that would have profited were the Seneca to lose title to this land.*

Outright non-Indian ownership of Seneca land under the city of Salamanca or in the "Congressional villages" was to be an elusive goal. In 1891, Congress passed a ninety-nine-year lease, which in effect extended earlier arrangements affirming non-Indian possession in the city of Salamanca and several "Congressional villages." At about the same time, the Seneca Nation launched a lawsuit, Appleby v. Seneca Nation, *which was designed to regain lands lost a century earlier when John Morris failed to pay for land in western New York known as the Morris Tract. The court, in a decision that would be unlikely to survive today, found that the non-Indian possession of the land was legal because so much time had passed.*

Congressman Edward B. Vreeland, a partner in the Seneca Oil Company and president of the Salamanca National Bank, led an effort to terminate and "allot" Seneca lands under a formula that would facilitate the transfer of Seneca lands to non-Indian hands. Although he was unable to get the kinds of bills he wanted, he and a small group of influential legislators sought bills that would transfer more control to the state in 1906, 1915, 1930, and 1940. This long and transparent campaign to transfer

Indian land to non-Indian hands helps explain, in part, Iroquois opposition to all kinds of change, including the 1924 Indian Citizenship Act and the 1934 Indian Reorganization Act.

One New York State legislative committee to investigate the Indian problem produced unexpected results. From 1919 to 1922 Chairman Edward Everett of Potsdam headed a committee which wrote a report finding that Iroquois Indians had been unlawfully defrauded of six million acres of land. The Everett Report was quickly and quietly buried in a bureaucratic wilderness, and Everett was shunned as a virtual traitor by other legislators. His assistant, Ms. Lulu Stillman, would later give a copy of the report to C. C. Daniels, who was then special assistant to the U.S. attorney general. Fred Forness, owner of a car dealership in Salamanca, was required to pay $4 per year for the use of the property under the terms of the Salamanca lease. He had not paid for eleven years. The general practice of Salamanca businesses and residents was to refuse to pay simply because the fee would cost more to collect than it was worth. C. C. Daniels recommended that the Seneca Nation cancel his and all delinquent leases, and the Justice Department agreed to champion the Seneca Nation in court.

The Forness case was finally settled on January 20, 1942, when a federal appeals court found in favor of the Seneca Nation. Salamanca residents at first refused to negotiate new leases at higher rates, but by 1944 most had agreed to renegotiated leases. The Seneca victory in the Forness case, however, set in motion a backlash against Indian rights and an attack on Indian property rights that would reverberate throughout the Iroquois country. Republican politicians in the city of Salamanca vowed revenge for the insolence of these Indians, and they turned to a friend in Congress, Senator Hugh Butler of Nebraska, for help.

The implications of the Forness decision was that New York State had less actual jurisdiction in Indian country within the state than had been previously thought. In response, the New York Legislature created the Joint Legislative Committee on Indian affairs in March 1943. It was dominated by members from the southwestern part of the state. By December two bills had been drafted that would transfer criminal and civil jurisdiction on Indian reservations from the federal government to New York State. The report of this committee, issued in February 1943, spoke almost entirely to the Salamanca lease situation. The mood in Washington was not helpful. In 1946, Commissioner of Indian Affairs Brophy was of the opinion that the BIA should be dismantled, and talk of "termination" was in the air.

"Termination" was more than a legal shift of federal responsibilities: it was a philosophy and a strategy of dispossession. "Termination" required legislation that

132

would change the status of Indian individuals and assets, which was then separate and distinct from the status of other Americans and which kept significant amounts of Indian assets out of the reach of the market economy and under federal protection. The "termination era" would end Indian status for 109 tribes composed of 13,263 individuals and involving 1,365,801 acres of land. Nebraska Senator Hugh Butler was a major figure in the termination movement. In a single year, 1947, he introduced bills to terminate Indian tribes in California, Montana, Wisconsin, Kansas, North Dakota, Oklahoma, and New York. Butler introduced three bills aimed at changing the status of the New York Iroquois.

The first contained language that would shift criminal offenses from federal to state jurisdiction; the second would transfer to New York courts jurisdiction over civil suits involving Indians; and the third would provide a lump sum payment to the Iroquois Indians to extinguish their rights under the Treaty of 1794. Although Butler and his allies in the termination movement were in no way sympathetic to Indian peoples or their rights, they couched their efforts in the language of emancipation and he once entitled a speech supporting termination "It Is Time to Give Serious Consideration to Setting American Indians Free." It was an action consistent with a time-honored American tradition of racial politics, which is to say one thing while meaning another.

The Iroquois were virtually unanimous in opposition to these laws. As often happens when a people's existence is at stake, there was a movement to revive ancient traditions. At Akwesasne, a political party ran for office on a ticket intended to dissolve the New York State-created elected system there and to replace it with traditional chiefs and to rejoin the political system of the ancient Confederacy. That party won, and New York State sent state police to conduct new elections, which were supported by the smallest of minorities. There were several exceptions to Indian unity on the issue of termination. Louis R. Bruce, Jr., a Mohawk destined to become head of the BIA in 1969, supported the termination bills. Moses White also approved. White was one of the staunchest supporters of the three-man elected council that had been created by New York State to endorse the state's claim to lands in the Mohawk country at the beginning of the nineteenth century. Nicodemus Bailey, leader of a faction representing an "elected system" on the Tonawanda Reservation near Akron, New York, also approved. These individuals, though a tiny minority, helped the Butler cause significantly.

Despite widespread Iroquois opposition, the criminal jurisdiction bill was passed in 1948. The Iroquois Confederacy unanimously opposed these bills and sent a spokesperson to express opposition to an amended civil jurisdiction act as late as September 9, 1950. The bill was signed on September 14. The Senate passed a version of the Senator Butler's bill to abrogate the Treaty of 1794 in 1949, but it never was signed into law. Butler died suddenly in 1954, ending the drive to terminate the Canandaigua Treaty of 1794.

In 1950 President Truman appointed Dillon S. Myer as Commissioner of Indian Affairs. He was best known for his wartime handling of Japanese Americans, who had been immorally imprisoned by the U.S. government in special camps, some of which were on Indian reservations. One of the "crimes" some of these people had committed was that they owned coveted agricultural land in the Pacific west. Powerful Anglo interests would use the anti-Japanese fervor created by the war to gain control of these lands. Dillon's new task would be to head a federal bureaucracy that was now in charge of physical assets and political futures of American Indian tribes, including the Iroquois.

American Indians had suffered in the patriotic fervor that followed most wars, but post-World War II was an especially difficult and dangerous time because of the Cold War atmosphere that engulfed the country. This cultural patriotism fostered a belief, on the one hand, that reservation life was somehow denying American Indians the benefits of rights and privileges of other Americans and, on the other, that reservation life sheltered Indians from responsibilities common to Americans in general. Both views supported efforts to "terminate" American Indian groups from federal supervision and, in the process, to take their homes and other real property from them. Congresswoman Reva Bosone of Utah introduced House Joint Resolution 490 in 1950, an initiative that required the BIA to designate tribes "ready" for termination. Such designations were to be proposed by January 1952, and Commissioner Dillon (along with other BIA officials) used this resolution to send a false signal to the Indian nations that termination was inevitable.

Two of the first groups chosen for termination were Iroquois: the Oneida of Wisconsin and the Seneca-Cayuga of Oklahoma. Events moved rapidly toward the total extinction of a long list of Indian groups and on August 15, 1953, Congress passed Public Law 280, which transferred from federal responsibility criminal and civil jurisdiction on Indian lands in California, Minnesota, Nebraska, Wisconsin, and Oregon in a move similar to the Butler bills of 1948 and 1950 in New York.

The Oneida of Wisconsin, led in their tribal Executive Council by Dennison Hill, Irene Moore, Charles A. Hill, and Mamie Smith, replied that what they needed was assistance in housing, education, and economic development programs, not termination legislation. The BIA stepped up its campaign to convince the Oneida to accept termination voluntarily with an offer of a $60,000 lump payment to terminate the Oneida interest in the 1794 Canandaigua Treaty. Commissioner Myer wrote Wisconsin Senator Joseph McCarthy that the BIA and the Oneida business council were jointly negotiating toward a termination result when in fact the Oneida had agreed to no terms of termination and were in no mood to discuss any. In December they voted 53 to 0 to reject the offer to abrogate their rights under the 1794 treaty.

Oneida unity in opposition to the abrogation of the 1794 treaty was disrupted by fierce intracommunity political struggles between the faction that had controlled the Tribal Executive Council (Tribal Business Committee) and a group of urban Oneida operating from Milwaukee and led by Oscar Archiquette and Morris Wheelock. Throughout this period (1953 to 1957) the Oneida consistently voted against any and all of the termination proposals. In the end, it may have been their poverty as much as their activism that allowed the Oneida to survive this period. Unlike the Menominee Nation of Wisconsin, which had significant forestry assets coveted by Wisconsin politicians and developers and were therefore prime targets for "termination," the Oneida held only 2,209 acres in Wisconsin, and the community possessed what can only be termed a remote chance at economic self-sufficiency. Wisconsin officials feared that termination would cost the state more money than would be realized, and termination of the Oneida slowly receded as an issue. The Menominee—the Oneida's neighbors—were not as fortunate. Termination would befall the

Menominee and would not be reversed until 1973.

Some Seneca and Cayuga had arrived during the 1820s and 1830s in Oklahoma as a result of removal and voluntary relocation policies. Most had subsequently migrated to other lands—a number of Cayuga had migrated to Grand River, Ontario country, while others settled at Seneca country in western New York. The Seneca and the Cayuga of Oklahoma merged in 1937 to take advantage of federal programs. In 1952 the BIA designated all of the Indian nations served by the Miami Agency as qualified for termination: the Eastern Shawnee, Modoc, Ottawa, Peoria, Miama, and the Seneca-Cayuga. Bitter internal squabbles hindered their struggle to survive during this period (1952 to 1957), but a BIA report advising that termination be delayed until all land claims were settled slowed the process.

Land claims, or more accurately, confusion around the status of numerous pieces of land, were a major factor in the delays which spared the Seneca-Cayuga the fate of other Indian nations in northeast Oklahoma. Other claims, such as the Cayuga rights to annuities under a 1788 New York Treaty and their case before the Indian Claims Commission Court added to the confusion and therefore to the delay in enacting termination. Chief Peter Bush, a Cayuga who had been born in the Grand River Country, was able to unite the factions into a successful stand against termination.

The Seneca-Cayuga Green Corn Festival and the tra-

ditional Iroquois culture played a significant role in the struggle against termination. Iroquois from as far away as the Mohawk country at Akwesasne attended the August 1957 event, as did Seneca from the Allegany Reserve and other Iroquois. These contacts brought news of the plans for the Kinzua Dam at Allegany and the taking of Mohawk land for the St. Lawrence Seaway and Tuscarora land for a proposed Robert Moses Power Project near Niagara Falls, New York. Menominees also arrived with accounts of the virtual rape of the Menominee Reservation and its forests, which had been facilitated by termination as a fait accompli. These contacts forged a sense of unity among many of these Iroquois. Most expected that Congress would enact termination acts even against Seneca-Cayuga wishes, but a strong opposition to the BIA and to federal initiatives to take from them their identity and their rights as Iroquois was rising in the Oklahoma communities. At a February 18, 1957, meeting in their council house, not a single member of the group voted in favor, and a significant majority voted against termination. Although the BIA would have preferred Indian acquiescence, Indian agent Paul Fickenger wrote then-BIA Commissioner Emmons recommending termination plans go ahead without Seneca-Cayuga consent. Emmons agreed, but was unable to get such a bill through Congress that year. The effort to terminate the Seneca-Cayuga ended in 1958 when a new secretary of the interior, Fred Seaton, announced that no

Indian groups would suffer termination without their consent.

The Seneca Nation in western New York faced termination and a threat to their lands from another direction as well: a $125 million public works project designated the Kinzua Dam, which proposed to flood more than 9,000 acres of land on the Allegany Indian Reservation. This project threatened to destroy the site of the Coldspring Longhouse, one of the main ceremonial centers of Seneca traditional life and to relocate 130 families. It would transform the Allegany Reservation from a rural community of scattered farms and homesteads along a riverway into two suburban communities, one at Jimmersontown near Salamanca and a second near Steamburg, New York. Seneca elder Harry Watt, responding to the prospect of rising waters over a beloved homeland, commented that when this flooding arrived, "that will be the sad, sad day."

The plan for the Kinzua Dam had been proposed in 1927. Seneca leaders opposed the dam from the start, but momentum for the project intensified during the years following World War II, coinciding with termination policy and the expanding public works initiatives under the Eisenhower administration. Historians generally credit the military style of President Eisenhower with removing much of the debate for construction of the dam from the public venue into the recesses of the administration's internal structure, the "back stairs" of the White House. Other agencies pressed for this project: the Pittsburgh Chamber of Commerce, the New York State Council of Parks, and most significantly, the Army Corps of Engineers. Pittsburgh industrialists representing Jones and Laughlin, Carnegie Steel, Gulf Oil, and H. J. Heinz Company lobbied for the dam as part of a flood control project that also addressed the issue of problems experienced by those corporations during low water periods during the summer. This corporate interest would later deflect alternative plans by the Seneca Nation and famed hydraulic engineer Arthur E. Morgan for flood control by diverting excess waters into the Conewango Valley without flooding the Allegany Reservation. The Army Corps of Engineers moved ahead with planning and preparations for the project even before Congress made final appropriations. They demonstrated singular insensitivity to Seneca concerns as they bulldozed sacred sites and refused to consider alternative sites for the Cornplanter cemetery.

People in the Indian Department during the Roosevelt administration had resisted attempts to build this dam, but Eisenhower's organizational genius overwhelmed all opposition. During this Republican administration the bureaucrats in the BIA expended extraordinary energy trying to convince Indian nations to accept termination voluntarily. They also managed a massive program to relocate as many Indians as possible to cities.

Cornelius Seneca, a respected iron worker and president of the Seneca Nation, was a leading figure during these years along with Wilfred Crouse, Theodore Gordon, Jr., Ernest Mohawk, and Adlai Williams. Seneca and the Seneca council mounted a well-designed campaign to stop the Kinzua Dam Project. They hired as their attorney Edward O'Neill, who had considerable experience under Aubrey Lawrence, head of the U.S. Department of Justice's Public Lands Division.

In 1956 the Seneca Nation hired Arthur E. Morgan, former director of the TVA and a leading civil engineer, to investigate alternatives to flooding the Allegany Reservation. He proposed construction of levies to divert flood-stage waters to a glacial depression in the Conewango Valley to the west of the Allegany Reservation. He claimed the plan would save Indian treaty rights while providing better flood protection and increased electricity generation capacity. Morgan enjoyed an international reputation and an ability to generate headlines, but he also had a long-standing feud with the Army Corps of Engineers, which did not assist him in this case.

In January 1957 the Department of Justice filed a condemnation proceeding at the insistence of the secretary of the army. Eight days later the Federal District Court for Western New York entered a finding that the Canandaigua Treaty of 1794 did not prevent the United States from taking Seneca lands for public works projects, a taking which that treaty appears to promise will never happen.

Hatfield Chilson, acting secretary of the interior, claimed that the 1948 and 1950 acts had in effect "terminated" federal responsibility in the Kinzua Dam matter.

Seneca Nation attorney O'Neill argued that the sanctity of a treaty such as that with the Iroquois Confederacy cannot be violated, as was happening in this case, by a pork barrel appropriation, that such a violation of treaty required a specific act of Congress to deal directly with the treaty issue. In retrospect, in the context of the moment, O'Neal's argument, that the Congress should be specific and show clear intent when it decides to undertake dishonorable activities against Indians, was playing against a stacked deck. Federal courts soon found that in simply passing the Appropriations Act of 1958 Congress had considered the 1794 treaty and had decided to violate it unilaterally. The final decision of a three-judge federal appeals court was rendered on September 25, 1958. It found that Congress had intended to violate the treaty, clearing away the final legal obstacle to construction of the Kinzua Dam.

Arthur E. Morgan's Conewango Alternative generated enough questions about whether the best plan had won the day that the head of the Army Corps of Engineers proposed hiring an "outside consultant" to compare the cost and engineering effectiveness of both the Kinzua Dam and the Conewango Alternative. They settled on the New York City engineering firm of Tippetts, Abbett,

McCarthy, and Stratten. This firm had numerous and intricate ties to the Army Corps of Engineers and did more business with the Corps than with any other customer. Despite these connections, their final report was surprisingly uncommitted, posing that both the Kinzua Dam plan and the Conewango Valley plan were feasible. Morgan's plan would cost more but would provide capacity for storing more flood water and for creating more electricity. It would require, however, moving four non-Indian hamlets. Western New York politicians' remarks at this time were revealing: there was no support for flooding non-Indian lands when Indian lands were available.

The Senecas mounted a powerful lobbying and public relations campaign. They enlisted the aid of anthropologist William N. Fenton, a classmate of New York Governor Nelson Rockefeller, to provide material about the importance of the 1794 treaty. Fenton successfully urged Edmund S. Wilson to take up the Seneca cause in his popular book With Apologies to the Iroquois. Brooks Atkinson defended Seneca rights in his column in the New York Times. Walter Taylor of the American Friends Services Committee lobbied tirelessly between 1961 and 1964. Well-known and respected anthropologist Stanley Diamond lent his support to the Seneca cause. Seneca Nation presidents Cornelius Seneca, George Heron, and Basil Williams spoke frequently and publicly of U.S. immorality in breaking the Canandaigua Treaty. Cornelius Seneca even appeared on a popular nationally televised game show, "To Tell the Truth."

On February 21, 1957, the Grand Council of the Iroquois Confederacy, the traditional government from which the Seneca Nation largely withdrew in 1848 and the political personality that signed the 1794 treaty with the United States, adopted a resolution condemning the proposed flooding of the Allegany Reservation and another reservation, the one-mile-square Cornplanter Grant further downriver inside Pennsylvania.

All of those efforts were to prove of no avail. General John Bragdon, Eisenhower's director of the White House Office of Public Works Planning, maneuvered the Army Corps of Engineers plans for the Kinzua Dam through the White House. Congress approved $1.4 million for the project in its 1960 budget, and Eisenhower added another $4.5 million to his 1961 budget. On June 23, 1960, while the Seneca Nation continued to press objections to the dam, Pennsylvania governor David Lawrence testified before James Haley's Subcommittee on Indian Affairs that the Indians would receive benefits that would "exceed by far" those they had received from the river since time immemorial. The last chance to stop the dam came with an appeal to President John F. Kennedy, who had made campaign utterances in support of Indian rights. Kennedy, however, owed significant political debt to the Pennsylvania political machinery of Governor Bradley. Kennedy declined to respond to Indian pleas for justice, thus joining a long line of U.S. presidents who had broken an Indian treaty and Indian hearts.

There was a history of resistance to erosions of Iroquois sovereignty in the Grand River Country during these years also. The Grand River chiefs had protested Canadian interference in their affairs throughout the nineteenth century. Following World War I, a delegation of chiefs went to Europe and tried to lay their grievance before the king of England and the League of Nations. One of these, Deskaheh, a Cayuga chief, insisted that the treaties between the Crown and the League were still in effect. In 1924 the Canadian police invaded the Grand River Country and seized its governing buildings. Canada replaced the traditional government with an elected system. Deskaheh was eloquent in his defense of his culture and his nation's rights to self-determination. He went on the radio and in public speaking halls in Europe and the United States to press his claim, but he died in exile, unable to reenter Canada because of Canadian reaction to his activism.

A Canadian version of "termination" resurfaced during the 1950s as did Haudenosaunee resistance. In March 1959, Iroquois traditionalists organized an effort to expel the elective system and to restore the Confederacy chiefs to power when they seized the council house at Ohsweken. The Royal Canadian Mounted Police raided the council house and reinstalled the elected government.

Court cases ensued that eventually affirmed the rights under Canadian law of the elected system, but with every effort at termination, the traditionalist faction returned with strength.

During the years of the Kinzua Dam controversy, three other Iroquois communities faced significant losses of land to development projects. The threat came in the form of a megadevelopment project designed to industrialize the St. Lawrence River Valley and to facilitate passage of deep-sea transport ships from the Atlantic to the western Great Lakes. The project, which came to be known as the St. Lawrence Seaway Project, was the product of agreements between the United States and Canada dating back to a 1909 treaty designed to expand hydroelectric production in the region dramatically.

Nature had rendered the St. Lawrence River largely impassable to deep-drought ships. By 1950, a series of canals and locks offered a 14-foot-deep channel considered inadequate for oceangoing vessels. The St. Lawrence Seaway Project was designed to change all of that. It would be the largest public works engineering project ever built and would involve the public treasuries of two countries. It would facilitate lifting ships 600 feet from the Atlantic and would enable large ships to pass from the Atlantic Ocean to Duluth, Minnesota—a distance of 2,350 miles and half a continent.

Standing in the path of this ambitious project were the

municipalities and rural areas of New York State that stood to be flooded by the project, plus three Iroquois communities: Tuscarora (near Niagara Falls, New York), Akwesasne (also known as St. Regis, near Cornwall, Ontario), and Kahnawake (known as Caughnawaga, near Montreal, Quebec). Construction began during the summer of 1954 with very little consultation with the Indians or consideration of Indian rights. Indian and non-Indian resistance to this project faced almost insurmountable odds.

Leading the project for Canada was attorney Lionel Chevrier. Although he was a resident of Cornwall, Ontario, and had lived near Indian people most of his life, he did not understand the Indian concerns or the concept of Indian nationhood or Indian rights. He viewed the Indians as people who were opposing the public good for strictly individual interests and seemed unable to grasp that the Mohawk interests and his view of Canada's interests in developing the Seaway were historically and intrinsically distinct. The Kahnawake community, located near Montreal, was in open rebellion against the project and felt it to be a clear violation of treaties and agreements with Britain and Canada dating back to the Proclamation Line of 1763. Kahnawake officials would try to take their case to the World Court and to the United Nations.

New York's Robert Moses, the most powerful bureaucrat in New York State (and probably in New York's history), masterfully managed the state's political system to pave the way for the project. Finally, the Eisenhower administration was driven by an ideological vision of development that was not significantly restrained by considerations about possible negative impact on communities, ecologies, or Indian rights. Moses had supported the Kinzua Dam Project and now supported the St. Lawrence Seaway. Arrogant, possessed with a sense of his own power, Moses had little appreciation for Indian rights. He had supported the Pittsburgh industrialists' demands for a dam at Kinzua as part of his political dealings, expecting reciprocal support in the future. He thought of Indian lands as sacrifice areas for his grandiose schemes for progress at the expense of poor and nonwhite peoples, and he treated the idea of Mohawk rights with an attitude of disdain. The result was that the Mohawk at Akwesasne, already incensed over the attack on their treaty rights under the 1794 treaty and the disregard of their opinions about the civil and criminal jurisdiction acts, emerged from this era with an increased sense of militancy and perhaps a potential for even greater factionalization than before.

In 1956 the Mohawk filed claim in the New York State Court of Claims for compensation for the taking of Barnhardt Island in the St. Lawrence River. Two years later the case was decided, and the Mohawk claim was rejected around technicalities involving border settlement agreements and an 1856 act of the New York Legislature, which purported to pay off Mohawk claims to that island.

In August 1957, some 200 Indians joined Frank Thomas (Standing Arrow) in an occupation of ancient Mohawk land in the Mohawk Valley off Route 5S on Schoharie Creek near Fort Hunter, New York. This was part of the protest for the unilateral taking of Mohawk land for the Seaway project. They were ordered off the land by a court in 1958, but this was the first in what would prove to be continuing protest actions by the Mohawk, who repeatedly moved from reserves to lands that had been taken from them in the late seventeenth century.

A part of the St. Lawrence Seaway Project involved taking 130 acres of Mohawk land on the Canadian side of Akwesasne. This led to increased friction. When the Canadian authorities erected tollbooths and tried to collect tolls from Mohawk, the protests escalated. When Canadian officials resumed their efforts to collect duties on goods carried by Mohawk living on Cornwall Island (in Ontario) and shopping in Massena, New York, Mohawk protesters parked their cars on the bridge and its approaches and let the air out of the tires. Forty Mohawk were arrested. In February 1969, there was another bridge blockade, and this time the Canadian government agreed to recognize the duty-free status of local Mohawk. The nationally known Indian newsmagazine Akwesasne Notes was created at the time of this blockade.

Niagara regional development, another of Robert

Moses' pet projects, confronted the Tuscarora Nation with the most serious challenge to its continued existence during this century. Moses' plans called for taking 550 acres of Tuscarora land as part of a power plant and reservoir project that would bear his name. The Tuscarora leaders, following a long-standing pattern of Iroquois resistance, declared themselves members of a sovereign Indian nation, stating that their lands could not be taken without their consent because of treaties with the United States. The Tuscarora under Chief Elton Greene hired the law firm of Strasser, Spiegelberg, Fried, and Frank and were assigned attorney Arthur Lazarus. Tuscarora activism intensified as Indians blocked access to Indian land with automobiles and tore up surveyors' stakes at night. It was during these protests that a young merchant seaman, who had never been a leader at Tuscarora and who never became one, came to the attention of the newsmedia. Wallace "Mad Bear" Anderson became one of the best-known participants, partly because of his profile in Edmund Wilson's book and partly owing to a flair for dramatic and sometimes outrageous publicity.

The Tuscarora people mounted increasing resistance, at one point shooting out the lights intended to make night work possible. There were arrests and unfavorable headlines. Moses caused the Indians' telephones to be "bugged," and the State Power Authority was able to bribe one of the Tuscarora chiefs for information. Moses eventually won the battle in the U.S. Supreme Court, where a majority of the judges concluded that the Tuscarora land was not protected by treaty because of a technicality. Edmund Wilson published articles in the New Yorker magazine supporting the Tuscarora case before the New York public. Moses retaliated with a pamphlet, "Tuscarora Fiction and Fact: A Reply to the Author of Memoirs of Hecate County and to his Reviewers." In the typical jargon of those whose intent was on taking Indian rights, Moses painted himself as a friend of the Indian who had only In- dian interests at heart. On August 12, 1960, the Tuscarora, finally admitting defeat, accepted an offer of $850,000 for 550 acres, but it was not a friendly settlement. Chief Clinton Rickard, who had led the fight for the rights of Indians to unimpeded crossing of the international border under rights guaranteed in the Jay and Ghent treaties between the United States and Great Britain, commented, "we were left with scars that will never heal."

The Oneida, meanwhile, were moving toward a new era. In 1966, an Oneida member, Robert Bennet, became commissioner of indian affairs. The Oneida Nation had been swindled out of millions of acres of land in New York, despite the fact that they had been staunch allies of the American revolutionaries and their fighting men had several times not only shown valor on the battlefield but arguably had tipped the tide. Their shabby treatment in the second and third decades of the nineteenth centuries certainly did not reflect the United States' debt to the Oneida, after the latter arrived with food during the winter, as Washington's troops were freezing and starving at Valley Forge.

Since the early 1950s the Oneida of New York worked tirelessly to obtain rights to sue to regain land and/or compensation for land and Indian political rights. Their arguments relied on gaining recognition in the courts that the federal Indian Non-Intercourse act of 1790 continued in effect and that the Oneida, whose land was taken without federal presence, could mount lawsuits in federal courts. On January 21, 1974, the Supreme Court unanimously agreed that the 1790 act was indeed in continued effect, a landmark decision which opened the way for Oneida and other Indians to press land claims in courts that had been previously closed to them.

National Indian politics arrived in the Iroquois country in the late 1960s. Mohawk people were part of the movements in the late 1960s, including the occupation of Alcatraz Island. The American Indian Movement, founded by urban Indians in cities such as Minneapolis, Minnesota, was gaining national attention as were other militant groups. In the summer of 1972, as the presidential election heated up, AIM launched what it called the Trail of Broken Treaties, a caravan to Washington to protest abuses of Indian rights. Representatives of the Trail of Broken Treaties arrived at Onondaga to report that they had inadvertently seized the BIA building and to request support. Significant numbers of Iroquois Indians joined the protests in Washington, which filled the newspapers and evening television around the United States and the world.

Following the BIA building occupation, AIM initiated an occupation at Wounded Knee, South Dakota, to call attention to abuses of Indians on one of the poorest Indian reservations in the United States. During this occupation, delegates from the Lakota Nation requested and were granted an agreement for mutual cooperation and assistance in what amounted to an Indian-nation-to-Indian-nation treaty of friendship with the Iroquois Confederacy.

In 1974 Mohawk from Kahnawake and Akwesasne organized the occupation of a former Girl Scout camp in the Adirondack Mountains near the hamlet of Eagle Bay. This set into motion significant activity by the New York authorities who surrounded the encampment. Several incidents involving gunfire so intensified the situation that New York authorities eventually agreed to relocate this Mohawk community, Ganienkeh, to lands near Plattsburgh, New York. It was the first instance in which Indians had regained land in New York as a result of activism.

In 1977 the Six Nations Confederacy was one of a number of nations that spearheaded an initiative organized by the Nongovernmental Organizations of the United Nations to attend a meeting at Geneva to propose international law standards to protect the rights of indigenous peoples worldwide. The Confederacy has maintained a significant presence in the deliberations, which have led to international legal standards concerning the rights of indigenous people and a proposed covenant on indigenous rights.

In 1979 serious disputes erupted in the Akwesasne Mohawk country when members of the "elective" system clashed with traditionalists. What began as a protest over the questionable arrest of a traditional chief escalated into charges when traditionalists demanded the mass resignation of a reservation police force and occupied elective system offices. The confrontation was to last for more than a year after traditionalists barricaded themselves in an encampment on Raquette Point. At one point, hundreds of New York State police faced hundreds of Indians in a very tense standoff. The criminal charges were eventually dropped, and the confrontation ended without solution.

In 1990 the Canadian town of Oka, Quebec, planned to build a golf course on land the Mohawk of Oka considered to be theirs. The Mohawk barricaded themselves on a road approaching trees slated for removal, and a tense standoff ensued. Eventually members of the Quebec Provincial Police stormed the barricade in a hail of gunfire. A police officer was killed, and the police retreated. Almost immediately, Mohawk supporters at the sister community of Kahnawake blocked the Mercier Bridge, a major artery between Montreal and its southern suburbs. Over the following months, Oka became the center of Canada's news interest and of native causes in Canada. The Confederacy sent a delegation and initiated negotiations with the Quebec government in an effort to end the confrontation. The effort was not successful, and the Canadian army eventually forced an end to the demonstrations.

Although there were serious threats to Haudenosaunee continued existence, and although it must certainly have appeared in 1946 that the Iroquois were doomed, the Iroquois are in fact growing in strength and influence in the 1990s, albeit not necessarily in unity. The Six Nations Council continues to meet at the Onondaga Longhouse near Nedrow, New York, and at the Onondaga Longhouse near Ohsweken. Its doors continue to be open to people who wish to use thinking instead of violence, just as the Peacemaker had hoped many centuries ago. As long as there are Iroquois Indians who are willing to place the good of the whole above the interests of the few, there will always be an Iroquois Confederacy.

John Mohawk